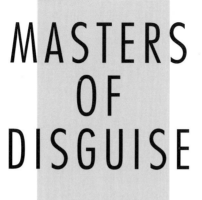

MASTERS
OF
DISGUISE

*The three-horned Jackson's chameleon, one of the most beguiling
of chameleon species, resembles a tiny triceratops.*

MASTERS OF DISGUISE

A NATURAL HISTORY OF CHAMELEONS

Text by James Martin
Photographs by Art Wolfe

Facts On File
New York • Oxford

Masters of Disguise: A Natural History of Chameleons

Text Copyright © 1992 by James Martin
Illustrations Copyright © 1992 by Art Wolfe

Facts On File, Inc   Facts On File Limited
460 Park Avenue South   c/o Roundhouse Publishing Ltd.
New York NY 10016   P. O. Box 140
USA   Oxford OX2 7SF
                                     United Kingdom

Library of Congress Cataloging-in-Publication Data
Martin, James, 1950-
Masters of disguise : a natural history of chameleons / James
Martin, Art Wolfe.
        p.   cm.
Includes bibliographical references and index.
ISBN 0-8160-2618-1
1. Chameleons. I. Wolfe, Art. II. Title
QL666.L23M365   1992
597.95—dc20   91-38050

A British CIP catalogue record for this book is available from the British Library.

Facts On File books are available at special discounts when purchased in bulk quan-
tities for businesses, associations, institutions or sales promotions. Please contact our
Special Sales Department in New York at 212/683-2244 (dial 800/322- 8755 except in
NY, AK or HI) or in Oxford at 865/728399.

Text and jacket design by Donna Sinisgalli
Composition by Facts On File, Inc.
Manufactured by Mandarin Offset
Printed in Hong Kong

10 9 8 7 6 5 4 3 2 1

To Terrie,

whose delight in the world's creatures is
contagious and enlivening.

CONTENTS

FOREWORD

Chameleons have long fascinated people with their color, shapes and behavior. They stand almost alone within their class: There are reptiles, and then there are chameleons.

Unfortunately, the chameleons' world is endangered and may disappear before these unique creatures fully reveal themselves to us. Habitat destruction, pollution and removal from the wild threaten their existence. And yet, ironically, when they are brought into our world for keeping, their beauty and vigor is only temporary, as few survive.

In recent years the Western world has seen an immense number of chameleons imported for the hobbyist and professional alike. Those of us fascinated with these lizards merely on an avocational level must deal with the frustration that accompanies a lack of appropriate resources.

Masters of Disguise offers us much more than the tidbits of information, scattered and scarce, which the chameleon enthusiast so greatly desires to find in a single source. What could previously be revealed only in the wild, hidden habitats of chameleons is now brought to light in this book, which combines the enthusiasm and wonder of the hobbyist with the accuracy and thoroughness of the specialist. With this book a chameleon renaissance has been born, and with it we continue to delve into their many mysteries, and bear the responsibility of maintaining their hidden world.

Ronald L. Tremper
Center for Reptile and
Amphibian Propagation

ACKNOWLEDGMENTS

This book wouldn't have been possible without the selfless assistance of many people. The folks at the reptile house at the San Diego Zoo spent several days with us and pointed us in the right direction. Todd Risley gave us access to his wonderful collection of living chameleons. James Naruo uncovered essential papers for me while visiting Madagascar. Enrico Cimader acted as an invaluable guide on Nosy Be to our group of befuddled Americans. Dr. Charles Crumly, at San Diego State University, and herpetologist Ronald Tremper permitted me to review scientific papers and provided me with invaluable comments. At the Seattle Zoo Dana Payne pointed me toward sources and Frank Slavens allowed me to rifle through what must be the largest private collection of herpetological literature in the country. Much of the value of the book comes from their kind assistance. Any inaccuracies are mine alone.

James Martin
Seattle

INTRODUCTION

"**H**ave you seen this lizard?"

My wife handed our neighbor a photograph showing a green, pop-eyed, three-horned, helmeted creature with one claw-like hand poised like a pointing retriever. "He's escaped," she said. The man stared at the picture, struggling to make sense of it. "He's very slow and hard to see," she explained. "Can you look at the tops of your bushes?" The man returned the photo to my wife. "Don't worry. Chameleons won't hurt you," she added. He didn't seem convinced.

Despite their fearsome appearance, it would be hard to design less dangerous creatures than Old World chameleons. Unlike the slim, green lizards kids buy at carnivals, which are actually American anoles, true chameleons look like antediluvian monsters. Their ability to change color and pattern is the least of their oddities. With independent eyeballs rotating like the turrets of a B-29, elaborate threat displays, prehensile tails, asymmetrically bundled toes, sloth-like pace, darting tongue and lolling gait—all wrapped in a baroque assemblage of crests, horns, helmets, flaps and frills—chameleons inspire mirth rather than menace.

People have been fascinated with chameleons for centuries. Chameleon bones are found with proto-human remains at Olduvai Gorge in Tanzania, and Africans and the Malagasy have created a battery of myths about them. "The natives really lost it if they see one," one safari guide explained to us. "They believe the devil made chameleons from spare parts: the tail of a monkey, the skin of a crocodile, the tongue of a toad, the horns of a rhinoceros, and the eyes of who-knows-what. Now the lizards spy on the world for their demon master. Once one appeared on a plant in my office, and my secretaries screamed and fled."

I've seen such fear in African eyes myself. While Art Wolfe photographed a diminutive chameleon, half a dozen Tanzanian youths surrounded him, wrinkling their noses and murmuring "kinyonga, kinyonga," Swahili for chameleon. At a safe distance they swaggered, carrying three-foot sticks as thick as axe handles, their usual defense against lions and buffalo haunting the rim of Ngorongoro Crater. But the sluggish lizard had them on edge. Every time the tiny kinyonga moved, they scattered in a panic, returning slowly with apprehensive smiles. When its tongue lassoed a fly, they let out a yelp like kids watching a horror movie. "Bad luck. Very dangerous," they warned, though one worldly native reassured us, "They look like they can do bad things, but they can't."

In one Pygmy myth set in the time before Man, when all was desert, a chameleon, hearing a whispering inside a tree, bored through the bark and water streamed out, bringing life to the world. In Central Africa a story is told of a protracted drought, when village elders sent a chameleon to persuade the gods to send rain to save the people; but the creeping reptile delivered the message after the villagers had already died. Today it's considered bad luck for women to look directly at a chameleon.

In Somalia people believe that a camel bitten by a chameleon will be barren. If a pregnant woman touches one, then her child, they say, will be born retarded, or "slow." In fact, a retarded child is called a chameleon. In most of Madagascar, killing a chameleon is "fady," or taboo. Drivers risk life and machine to avoid running over a chameleon crossing the road. In the north many believe that any injury you inflict on the tiny *Brookesia* chameleon will soon happen to you.

Luckily for the species, most myths surrounding chameleons imbue them with supernatural powers, not utility or commercial value. Unlike the rhinoceros, the chameleon needn't fear its horns will attract hunters in search of aphrodisiacs or dagger handles. However, Moroccan pharmacists sell dried chameleon as a medicine, and East Africans consider cutting off a horn to be a sign of great courage.

Our own escapee was a Jackson's chameleon, indigenous to the highlands of Kenya and Tanzania. Strutting about with goofy solemnity, three horns sprouting from his armored skull, he resembled a shrunken triceratops. Not all chameleons grow horns; some manage only a vestigial stump while others glory in four fully developed horns.

The Jackson's demeanor is mostly bluff. If you put your finger in his open mouth, he won't bite. His eyes rotate as he decides how to extricate himself from this situation. (Don't try this with the larger Malagasy species—the panther chameleon chomps at the first opportunity.) Among the Jackson's virtues, intelligence is not the most prominent. Several times I've seen a male grab his own horn while climbing. A panicked struggle ensues as he tries to escape from himself.

My wife and I found a pair of Jackson's confined to a small aquarium in a California pet store. Their outrageous appearance and erratic movements fascinated us. Even though we had no idea what the creatures needed, it was clear to us the pet shop employees were even further at sea. Crickets roamed the cage, and lettuce sat in a bowl untouched. With the prehensile tail and feet designed for gripping, they were obviously arboreal lizards, but no branches had been provided for them. They sat in the corners, repetitively scratching on the glass with one arm, eyes rotating. Day by day a bowl of water evaporated. It turns out that Jackson's drink only by lapping water droplets off a leaf. We visited the shop daily for a week before we snapped. We paid the bail and sprung them.

No information about the habits and needs of our pets seemed to exist. We relied on hearsay, inference and much anthropomorphizing. Scraping on the glass of their cages denoted a demand for freedom, we figured. They always climbed to the top of any houseplant so they desired altitude. Apparently, they adhere to the New Hampshire motto, "Live free or die," so we accommodated them by stringing ropes from our ceiling, creating lizard highways. Given the run of the house, they preferred to commute from wall to wall on the ropes, veering only to the curtains to bask in sunbeams. And they had one trait any parent would envy. Both fell asleep one minute after we switched off the lights.

They flourished. We rejoiced. But soon they lost all desire for crickets, their staple diet. Mealworms rekindled their appetite, but boredom soon set in. My wife and I could be found on sunny days crawling around our yard looking for tasty invertebrates, as our fussy eaters sunned themselves in the garden. We tried to shoo away bees and wasps, but the Jackson's still hunted them. After zapping a bee, they would sit with their mouths open, like an incautious diner at a Thai restaurant. (Some species bite the stinger off before swallowing; others avoid stinging insects altogether.) The population of spiders and flies dwindled around our house that year.

The chameleons revealed their authentic personalities outdoors. In the California summer we rigged a chicken wire cage and left them outside 24 hours a day. They rocked on branches, avoiding detection by moving with determined indecision. A passing bird or plane froze them in position, one eye turret tracking the threat. These happy days didn't last. Eventually they died, causes unknown. Of six Jackson's we adopted, only one lived over two years in our care. Determined to avoid such heartbreak in the future, we plunged into the literature on chameleons, where we discovered a morass of conflicting views and incompatible "facts."

Reading about chameleons confused us until we realized the range of physiology and behavior this family of lizards displays. Egg-layers require different conditions than chameleons that give live birth. Our Jackson's would have died their first day in the desert the Namaquas call home, while a Namaqua would fall to its death trying to imitate a Jackson's aerial maneuvers. Almost any statement regarding chameleons can be contradicted by at least one member of the family. For most chameleon species science is silent regarding diet, lifespan, breeding behavior and the language of color. The deeper we penetrated their world, the more we recognized that much of the lives of chameleons remains a mystery.

THE
CHAMELEON
BASICS

Almost all chameleons live in Africa or Madagascar, but the European chameleon and related subspecies range into Spain, Palestine, Arabia, India and Sri Lanka. In Africa they inhabit the rain-saturated jungles of the Congo Basin, the desiccated wastes of the Namib Desert and the roses of Nairobi's parks. Some species survive rare snowfalls on the continent's equatorial peaks. Most chameleons belong to the genus *Chamaeleo*, but about one-fifth are *Brookesia* or *Rhampholeon,* the latter also called stumptail chameleons or leaf chameleons for their resemblance to dead leaves. As their name implies, stumptails do not possess the effective prehensile tail that other chameleons wrap around tree branches and live their lives entirely on the ground. Their range of color is restricted too. Most are brown and darken when threatened, perhaps adding

Nearly all chameleons live in Africa or Madagascar,
although the range of some species extends to Spain,
Palestine, Arabia, India and Sri Lanka.

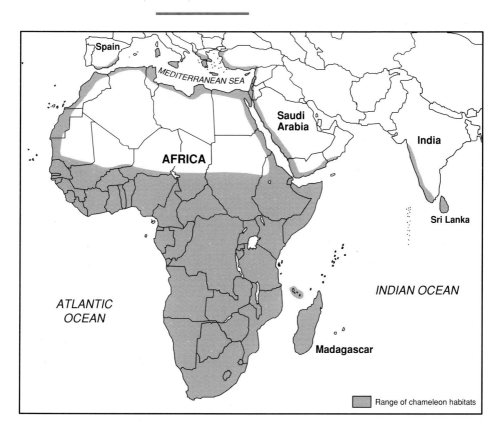

a bit of green or yellow if thrown into a tizzy, but they cannot rival the displays of their fully arboreal brethren.

Arboreal chameleons rarely visit terra firma. No other creature seems so well adapted to life in the branches. Most species spend the bulk of their day the color of bark or leaves, an effect magnified by their flat ovoid shape. They rock back and forth as they walk, like a leaf in the breeze, often waiting for wind to stir the branches before moving. The prehensile tail stretches straight for balance when the animal is walking and winds itself around a branch for security when the chameleon is feeding or making a tricky maneuver. When feeling secure or showing off, chameleons curl it in a tight spiral. I once saw one catch a branch with his tail after freefalling several feet. Each foot forms a "V," with front and back toes bundled together for stability and strength. Front feet have two toes bundled on the outside, three on the inside; the rear feet have the opposite arrangement. If disturbed while sleeping, some species reflexively drop to the ground, eluding capture by a snake or bird. Babies and smaller species often jump when approached—and land like a bag of groceries.

Watching a chameleon walk on the ground is an entertaining way to spend an afternoon. They walk on the tips of their claws, feet splayed wide, reptilian pianists playing octaves. The gait that effectively masks their presence on a bush takes on a goofy, conspicuous character on land, which serves only to draw attention, not to conceal. Even when fleeing in panic, they cover less than 20 feet a minute. Exposed, they possess no defense against predators except a truly pathetic bluff: Their throats expand, they stand tall, and open their mouths. This could impress a fellow chameleon, but the threat is lost on vipers and shrews.

THE CHAMELEON FAMILY TREE

Four orders of reptiles remain on Earth, cold-blooded remnants from the reptile heyday in the Mesozoic age, more than 200 million years ago. Most reptiles, over 6,000 species, belong to the Squamata order, and more than half are lizards. The other three orders include less than 250 species: 225 turtles (order Chelonia), 21 crocodilians (order Crocodilia) and New

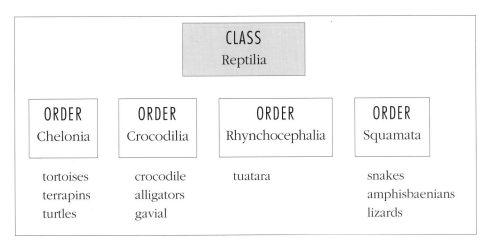

The chameleon's relationship to other reptiles.

Zealand's primitive tuatara (the only surviving species from the Rhynchocephalia order). Lizards comprise the Sauria suborder of the Squamata order, which they share with snakes (suborder Ophidia) and amphisbaenians (suborder Amphisbaenia)—legless burrowing reptiles.

Chameleons are lizards. Lizards differ from their cousins the snakes by possessing movable eyelids and four legs. The so-called legless lizards retain their limb girdles, vestiges of their days as quadrupeds.

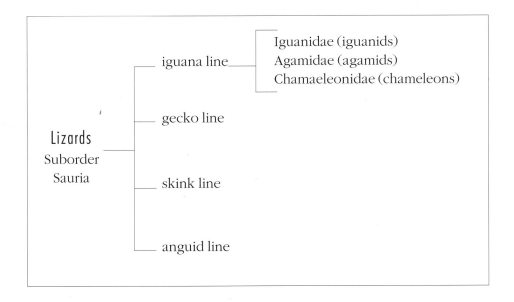

The chameleon uses its prehensile tail to grasp onto tree branches. When the chameleon is relaxed or showing off, it may curl the tail into a tight spiral.

Within the Sauria suborder, over 100 species belong to the Chamaeleonidae family of lizards. A species is defined as a group of animals capable of reproducing. Species evincing similar traits, believed to have sprung from common ancestors, are grouped together in genera. Chameleons are divided into two to four genera, depending on the authority consulted. Most chameleons belong to the genus *Chamaeleo*.

The Chamaeleonidae family has been considered as being related to the Agamidae because of similar circulatory systems and acrodont dentition (teeth firmly soldered to the jawbone). The chameleons of the world share only two characteristics to separate them from their scaly siblings: independent eyes and an extensible tongue for feeding. The number of other structures and behaviors encompassed within Chamaeleonidae beggars belief. Many dwarf species lack usable prehensile tails or the ability to change color significantly. Horns occur in a minority of species, and foot structure differs. Most lay eggs, but several montane species and South African dwarf chameleons deliver live young. Some tiny representatives lurk under a cover of leaves on the forest floor while their larger cousins sun on the canopy above. Size ranges from a few centimeters to almost 3 feet.

While scientists all agree on the above characteristics that qualify a lizard for inclusion in the Chamaeleonidae, the way in which chameleons are related to one another has become a noisy arena where competing theories battle for acceptance. Rival taxonomies—classification systems defining genus, species and relationships—attract defenders and revisionists. The best answers would convincingly explain chameleon phylogeny—their evolutionary development—and geographic dispersal. So far, the picture is muddled and incomplete.

The chameleon's bundled toes give it a firm grasp on branches as it walks through the treetops.

To define genus and species, herpetologists compare and contrast anatomical features, from the shape of skull and scales to the number of horns and protuberances, from the lengths of tails to the presence of tarsal spurs (thorn-shaped hooks behind the rear leg). They redraw the chameleon family tree according to the relative complexity of lung structure or the number of chromosomes. Even the baroque variations of chameleon hemipenis morphology, startling with their unearthly, vegetative shapes, serve as evidence in the debate.

Early African explorers established the first classification systems for chameleons. In the late 19th and early 20th centuries the Belgian zoologist George Boulenger tramped through the jungles and forests of equatorial Africa cataloging plants and animals. Expeditions to Madagascar expanded his collections. In some cases the specimens he brought back are the only existing examples of rare species. Along with the German Albert Gunther and other intrepid curiosity seekers and inveterate classifiers, Boulenger helped establish the first tentative classification system to bring order to this confusing family.

Sorting chameleons into genera is a chancy business. Any one assertion will meet several objections. The first scientists established two genera, *Chamaeleo* and *Brookesia*. Members of *Chamaeleo* look like true chameleons and comprise three-quarters of all species. Prehensile tails extend to at least as long as the body. Opposing bundled toes act as pincers for gripping, and smooth-scaled soles provide traction. The body is laterally flattened so at first glance the arboreal lizard looks like a leaf. *Chamaeleo* covers the entire geographical range of Chamaeleonidae. While most species lay eggs, some give live birth.

From the first, however, taxonomists recognized that stumptail or Pygmy chameleons deserved a separate branch. This category of tiny, ground-dwelling *Brookesia* chameleons seem quite different from their larger, arboreal cousins, but no single common characteristic separates them from every member of *Chamaeleo*. They tend to be small and squat, with triangular-shaped skulls. They retain the pincer feet, but the soles are spiny rather than smooth, and the short tail has limited prehensile ability. Their color repertoire is limited and all lay eggs. The Jacobson's organ, which is found on the roof of a reptile's mouth and aids in the sense of smell, is lacking. (The tongue darts into the air and returns to the mouth bearing molecules for the Jacobson's organ to recognize.) The organ is vestigial in most chameleons.

Most herpetologists now divide stumptail chameleons into two genera, the *Brookesia* of Madagascar and the *Rhampholeon* of Africa, but other characteristics divide the Pygmies. *Brookesia* are terrestrial, living among the leaves of the rain forest floor, while the continental *Rhampholeon* live in brush and undergrowth. *Rhampholeon* toes have unique bicuspid (with two points) claws. Hemipenis structure differs in details. Because the African Pygmy or dwarf chameleons more closely resemble arboreal chameleons, phylogenists theorize that *Brookesia* descended from African *Rhampholeon*-like ancestors.

After establishing the primary divisions, scientists looked for ways to distinguish species and subspecies. They noted great diversity in skull morphology, especially crests and casques, so many studies concentrated on charting cranial differences.

CHAMELEON ANATOMY

Learning the herpetologist's jargon focuses attention on the markers defining species and subspecies. Like Adam's power to name the animals, we gain dominion over a discipline by naming things. Unlike the cloudy jargon of the social sciences, where inflated synonyms elbow out serviceable English, natural science terms act as shorthand for complex descriptions. It's easier to say "gular crest" than to say "a line of scales frilled perpendicularly under the throat." Anyone interested in chameleons will soon find words like "squamation" and "scia dentata" rolling trippingly off the tongue. (A glossary of these terms is provided at the end of this volume.)

On following page:
With its small size and shorter tail, the stumptail chameleon little resembles its larger, more colorful relatives.

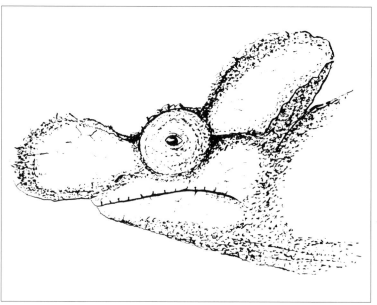

The shape and size of the casque and facial protuberances vary among chameleon species. C. carpenteri *is illustrated at top,* C. xenorhinus *below.*

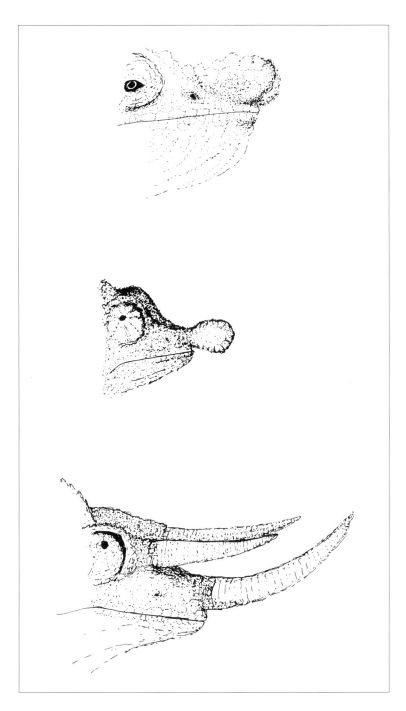

A variety of facial appendages. Shown from the top are the rigid, bifurcated appendage of C. parsonii, *the flexible, laterally compressed appendage of* C. nasatus *and the three annulated horns of* C. jacksonii.

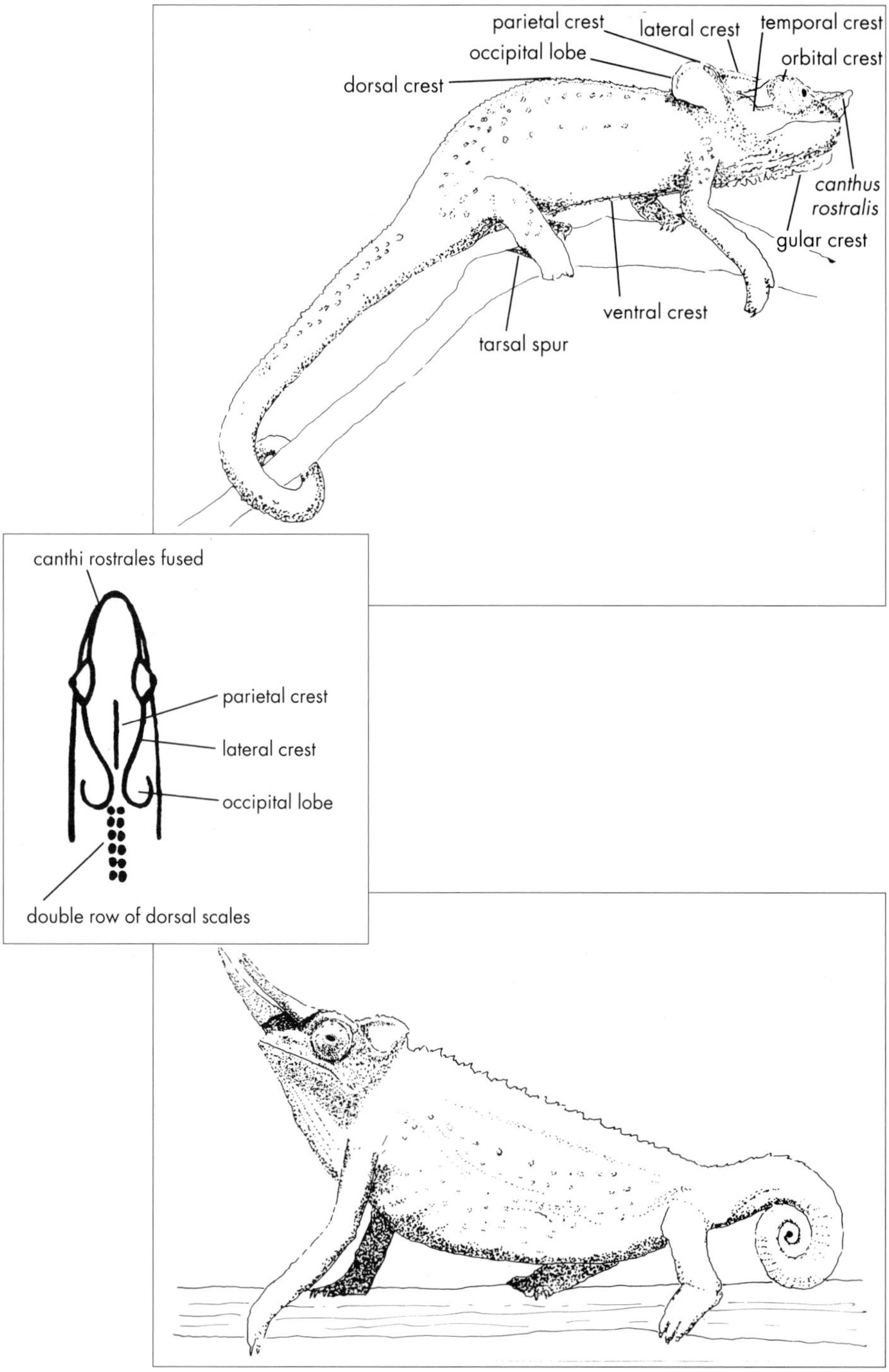
parietal crest
lateral crest
temporal crest
occipital lobe
orbital crest
dorsal crest
canthus
rostralis
gular crest
ventral crest
tarsal spur
canthi rostrales fused
parietal crest
lateral crest
occipital lobe
double row of dorsal scales

The shape of different crests, casques and lobes is used to identify chameleon species. A generic chameleon is above, C. jacksonii *below.*

When the head of a chameleon rises noticeably above its neck, it is said to have a casque. Some casques require a second look to discern, while others more than double the height of the skull. Larger casques may make males look more formidable to opponents. Some scientists speculate that the giant casques of the Yemenese *calyptratus* collect dew in the morning for drinking water in Yemen's arid hills and that the reptile stores fat in the head to hedge against lean times.

C. calyptratus *boasts one of the most impressive casques of all chameleon species.*

Bony crests encircling the casque or bisecting its top are called lateral and parietal crests, respectively. The parietal crest can bulge forward like the bow of a ship, curve back like a scythe or barely disturb the surface of the skull. Oddly shaped scales often festoon lateral crests. A protruding ring of bone harbors the eye. A crest running toward the snout is called a canthal crest. In some cases, as with the Parson's chameleon, the canthal crests erupt into dramatic rostral appendices or protuberances.

While the chameleon's ability to change color is its most remarkable feature, the canvas for the reptilian artist's dermal painting—a hide consisting of bumps, scales, crevices and frills—evokes almost equal astonishment. The word squamation, from the same root as the Squamata order, means the arrangement of scales, which is one characteristic herpetologists use to distinguish species. Scales are areas of thickened skin that vary in size and shape. Some overlap like shingles while others are mere granules.

Like other lizards, chameleons shed their skin. Because they grow rapidly, young chameleons shed their skin more often than adults. As the animal grows, the skin on the surface dies. The new skin breaks through the old, and soon the chameleon looks tattered, as sheets of dead, white skin flutter in the breeze. Shedding can block vision and impede hunting when the eyelids and snout peel. The lizards can be seen rubbing their eyes against bark to strip them clean. Sometimes

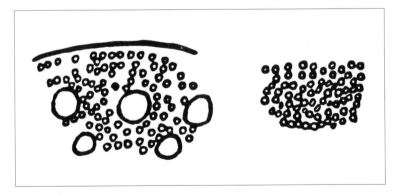

The squamation, or arrangement of scales, varies among chameleon species. Illustrated here are a variety of scale patterns.

the entire shed torso of the animal remains intact, resembling the white ghost of a chameleon. Chameleon scales sprout into leafy or toothy adornments also called crests (not to be confused with the bony ridges that subdivide chameleon skulls).

Enlarged ovoid scales called tubercles often decorate the sides of the body or the top of the head, placed randomly or in lines. Sometimes groups of similar scales form rosettes or other patterns. Large, smooth and pale scales, dubbed scia dentata, mimic teeth to give the reptile a fearsome appearance, at least to other chameleons. A lizard exhibiting evenly distributed equal-sized scales is said to possess homogeneous squamation. More often, heterogeneous squamation prevails, and patterns comprised of differing scales complement the chameleon's colors. Often the brightest tints appear on conspicuous tubercles, stippling the lizard's flanks. Mapping the vagaries of chameleon skin is another tool for identifying species.

Scientists also use scale crests to distinguish between similar species and to define subspecies. For example, the only significant difference between *C. lateralis* and *C. lambertoni* is the presence of a fringe of scales under the neck of lateralis, a gular crest. The dorsal crest of *C. parsonii christifer*, a row of scales along its back, separates it from its otherwise identical smooth-backed brethren, *C. parsonii.* The shape and order of the fringe scales comprising a crest can also be helpful in identifying chameleon species. Are the scales hook-shaped or tabular, short or long? Are all the scales the same size or does a repeating pattern show itself? Do the scales align in a single row or a double row or do they interleave?

Near the turn of the century, Werner guessed that many chameleon characteristics, such as horns or occipital lobes, evolved independently within segregated chameleon populations undergoing parallel evolution. Most taxonomists studying chameleons accept Werner's hypothesis of parallelism. Chameleons developed similar structures in different places and at different times, distinguishing between primitive and recently

On following page:
Like snakes, chameleons shed their skin periodically. Here, a
female Jackson's is shedding.

developed characteristics will be difficult without corroborative evidence.

In the 1970s and 1980s, the biologist Charles Klaver and the late Dutch taxonomist Dirk Hillenius quarreled in the scientific press over the most accurate description of chameleon heritage and species relationships. Instead of slashing their way through jungles and brambles, they worked in laboratories trying to assemble coherent explanations of how chameleons developed and dispersed. They redrew the family tree and proposed candidates for the closest relative to the original chameleon and tried to locate the Olduvai Gorge of Chamaeleonidae.

Because 40% of genus *Chamaeleo* appear on Madagascar, one could argue that the island launched the distribution of the genus. However, every characteristic found among the Madagascar species is found on the continent but not vice versa. No Madagascar chameleons give live birth, grow cranial horns or develop tarsal spurs, yet these variations appear across Africa in diverse habitats.

These observations were used to establish a sequence of evolutionary change. It is often assumed that more complex structures originated later than simpler ones. For example, horns were likely a comparatively recent evolutionary event. Hillenius looked at these external clues and reasoned that the species with the fewest adaptive characteristics and the widest distribution would represent the trunk of the family tree, leading back to the mother of all chameleons. By his criteria, he concluded that *Chamaeleo chameleon* was the closest relative of the early chameleon. Except for tarsal spurs near the feet, it is one of the least adorned, lacking occipital lobes, horns, crests or other decorations. Its scales are all the same size. This lizard and its close cousin, the occipital lobe-equipped *dilepis*, range from southern Africa to the shores of the Mediterranean Sea. The chameleons of the Middle East and India are close kin. Hillenius reasoned further that the district with the greatest number of characteristics scattered across all species would qualify as the epicenter of chameleon evolution. He concluded that the agonizingly slow dispersal and evolution of the Chamaeleonidae originated in East Africa.

Arguing from shared physical traits, the same method used by the earliest researchers, his taxonomy charted the relation-

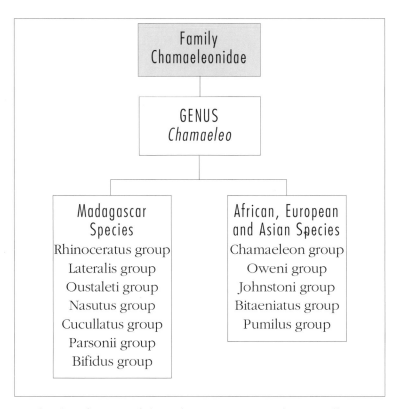

The classification of chameleon species according to Hillenius.

ships among groups of similar lizards and species within a group. For example, he believed *Chamaeleo xenorhinus*, a resident of the Ruwenzori Mountains of Uganda and Zaire, is a close relative of Madagascar's *rhinoceratus* group, based primarily on the similarity between their rigid, laterally compressed rostral appendices. His taxonomy connected other widely dispersed species using similar evidence. He examined pickled specimens explorers had been bringing back since the 19th century, elevating some to species status and demoting others to mere subspecies. An analysis of chromosome counts appeared to confirm most of his family groupings. Hillenius rearranged the extant classification system, confining his modifications to redefining species.

Klaver looked to lung and hemipenes structures to confirm Hillenius's vision of the chameleon family tree. He assumed that lizards with simpler lung structure, lungs with fewer subdividing septa, most closely resembled ancestral chameleons. In

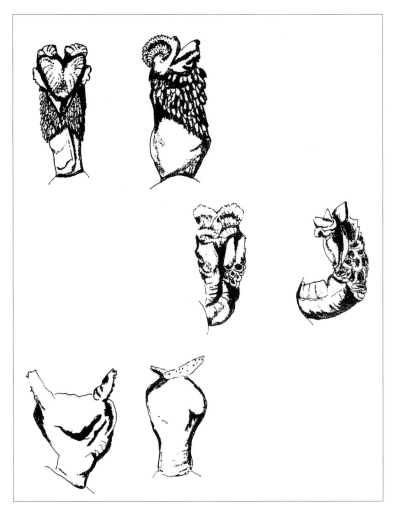

The hemipenes, or twin penises, of chameleons may have an elaborate adornment of ridges, crests and horns.

general, his new evidence corroborated Hillenius's work, but Klaver found a plague of nits to pick.

Hillenius had rejected the assumption of adaptive value. If a species developed a characteristic that had no apparent survival benefits, Hillenius concluded that no benefits existed, while Klaver assumed the utility was merely unclear, not absent. Klaver took his colleague to task for defining some characteristics as primitive and of ancient origin without a supporting argument, discerning an ad hoc quality in Hillenius's conclusions. "They explain the observed facts very nicely, because they were made

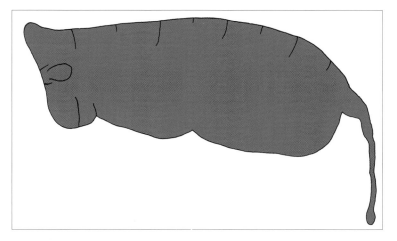

An illustration of the simple lungs of C. aldolfifrederici *which indicate a more primitive level of development for the animal, according to Klaver.*

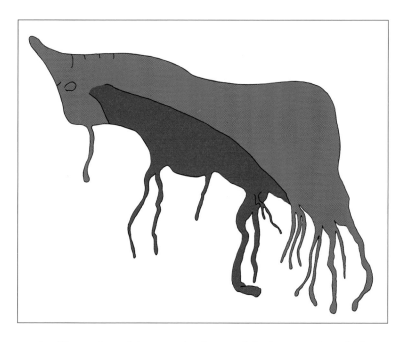

An illustration of the complex lungs of C. deremensis, *which indicate a more evolved animal, one further along the evolutionary path, according to Klaver.*

to do so," he wrote in harsh language for the halls of academe. Citing anomalies in penis and lung structures, Klaver found fault with both Hillenius's methodology and conclusions. Hillenius had grouped chameleons of similar appearance together without regard to geographic separation. Klaver scoffed at Hillenius's contention that some widely dispersed chameleons were closely related. Hillenius's placing of *xenorhinus* among the *rhinoceratus* group of Madagascar chameleons left Klaver sputtering. How the lizard rafted across the Mozambique Channel, crossed a thousand miles of arid plains and hiked into the rainy forests high on the slopes of the Mountains of the Moon without pausing to set up colonies along the way was not explained. Klaver showed that the internal characteristics of the separated groups argued against the close relationships Hillenius assumed.

Klaver's focus on penis and lung morphology wasn't arbitrary. Chameleons possess more complex lung structures than other lizards, and researchers have long depended on penis morphology to identify snakes. The penis of lizards and snakes is paired, each side called a hemipenis. A pair of propulsor muscles extrude the hemipenes out through the cloaca (the reptile's all-purpose excretory and reproductive orifice), and blood fills erectile tissue sinuses. When erection is complete, one hemipenis enters the female. Ducts from the testes secrete sperm on to the male cloaca, and the sperm flows along grooves on the hemipenis surface. Of all reptiles, chameleons have the most elaborate hemipenes topology, an exotic terrain of lips, crests, horns, scoring and papillae for sperm to traverse.

In his seminal paper in association with German biologist Wolfgang Böhme, "Phylogeny and Classification of the Chamaeleonidae with Special Reference to Hemipenis Morphology," Klaver unified a chaotic nomenclature. He collapsed the fanciful French terms—*réseau de cellules polygonales, alvéoles polydriques* and *réseau alvéolaires*—to the more prosaic *calyces* to indicate ornamentation midway along the hemipenis. Using his streamlined terminology, he grouped chameleons according to hemipenes ornamentation.

The lungs of the various chameleon species differ distinctly. In some species the lungs extend virtually throughout the body, allowing the chameleon to puff up for defensive and courting displays. Some have smooth, undivided lungs while others possess complex, partitioned ones. Klaver concluded that simple lungs implied a primitive level of development while complexity indicated a more evolved animal. The simpler the lung, the closer to the state of the ancestral chameleon.

Klaver's studies led him to reject the *Chamaeleo chameleon* as the chameleon Eve. Despite relatively few external characteristics and its wide distribution, the complexity of its lungs and hemipenes argued against its early origin. To Klaver, members of Hillenius's *pumilus* family exhibited the characteristics his theory predicted an ancient chameleon would possess. Alone among chameleons, they possess undivided lungs. Their vestigial Jacobson's organ is more developed and is positioned in the mouth as if it still functioned, suggesting the group recently abandoned its use. Unlike the other members of genus *Chamaeleo*, they feature a thickened parietal bone, but not with the distinctive triangular skull shape or limited prehensile tails of *Brookesia* and *Rhampholeon*, and give live birth.

Some herpetologists, mostly South African, had already proposed a new genus for the *pumilus* group, dubbing them *Microsaura* or *Lophosaura* or *Bradypodion*. *Bradypodion*, meaning "slow foot" in Latin, became the accepted name. Klaver agreed the *pumilus* deserved separation from the rest of *Chamaeleo*, and he included several species from outside South Africa in the group.

With the *Brookesia*, Klaver's criteria runs into further difficulties. If they evolved from an early chameleon and are in the process of abandoning arboreal features, one might expect to find complex lung and hemipenis structures, but both are simple. Klaver postulates that the advantages of complex lung structure are relevant only in arboreal species. As they lose unnecessary lung complexity and prehensile tail from disuse, *Brookesia* in effect practice reverse evolution.

Klaver, too, succumbed to the temptations of unsupported assertion. Apparently carried away by the spirit of revisionism, he wrote, "Although we do not know the hemipenis morphology of. . . .*C. xenorhinus* we expect it to be very different for the one found in *C. rhinoceratus*." Then he renders his verdict. "The relationship assumed by Hillenius is, therefore, refuted."

Klaver concluded the two Chamaeleonidae genera, *Chamaeleo* and *Brookesia*, qualify as subfamilies. *Chamaeleo*, renamed Chamaeleonidae, would contain four genera: *Chamaeleo*, *Bradypodion*, *Furcifer* and *Calumma*. *Brookesia*,

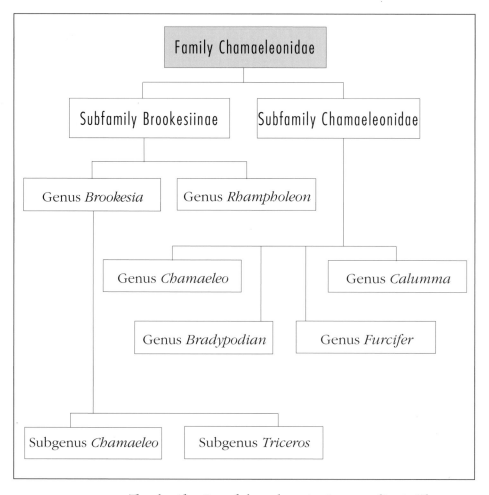

The classification of chameleon species according to Klaver.

now sub-family Brookesiinae, would be divided according to location and divergent hemipenes structure, *Brookesia* in Madagascar and *Rhampholeon* in Africa.

Both Hillenius and Klaver saw chameleons through the lens of their own systems. For Hillenius, a simple surface denoted a primeval structure. For Klaver, undivided lungs and unadorned hemipenes provided the most significant clues for assigning primitive status. By limiting their investigations to just a few characteristics, they reduced their opportunities to establish the definitive chameleon family tree.

In the late 1980s new evidence cast doubt on both Hillenius and Klaver's systems. Frost and Etheridge (1989) recognized chameleons as a subfamily of an expanded Chamaeleonidae family. The related subfamilies include the Agaminae and Leiolepinae. Dr. Charles Crumly of the University of California, San Diego, agreed and found Klaver and Böhme's reorganization of Chamaeleonidae flawed. He examined external anatomy, osteology, hemipenial structure, the microscopic structure of scales and developmental anatomy. Dr. Crumly's evidence doesn't support Klaver and Böhme's reorganization.

Despite the passion of the debate, the evolutionary path of chameleons is still clouded. However, because a description of lung and penis morphology or a list of chromosome counts would be of little use to someone trying to identify a living specimen, this book adheres to traditional nomenclature used by Hillenius, despite its weaknesses. (Appendix I provides detailed information on chameleon taxonomies.)

While creating taxonomic systems is entertaining and illuminating to a point, chameleon behavior remains virtually a blank page. Because each species performs a unique combina-

A Parson's chameleon zaps its prey. The lightning-fast tongue can extend to one-and-a-half body lengths in one-sixteenth of a second.

tion of courting and threatening behaviors—pattern changes and posturing used to communicate with other members of their species—behavior may be the most accurate way to classify chameleons. The lizards themselves know who their cousins are and respond appropriately. Only a handful of studies have concentrated on observation in the field so far. After a lifetime of studying the creatures, Hillenius noticed that male and female pairs stayed together for months at a time, often within a meter of each other. If this simple fact escaped a century of chameleon studies, a mother lode of discoveries likely awaits researchers willing to spend their working lives in the bushes instead of the laboratory.

THE SENSES

Evolution has produced thousands of survival strategies, but none more amazing than the chameleon's tongue. Once an insect blunders within range, the lizard conducts a series of operations that would be the envy of any gunnery squad, sighting, aiming and firing with speed and accuracy.

To gain mastery of the tongue, the lizard has had to sacrifice other abilities. You'll never thrill to the call of wild chameleons. The best they can manage is a faint hiss. Even if they could warble like songbirds, their neighbors wouldn't notice. Among reptiles, chameleons have the poorest hearing, excepting only one species of lacerta from Persia. Shouting next to a sleeping chameleon won't rouse him, and even when awake they disregard most sounds. However, they respond to ground- or branch-borne sound. Blindfolded desert chameleons hiss in the direction of rocks dropped near them.

In place of the ear opening, a membrane of skin on the side of the skull called the auditory area registers airborne vibrations and transmits them to a delicate bony structure called a pterygoid plate. Embedded in tissues within the skull, the plate relays the vibration down a twisting and constricted pathway leading to the inner ear. Compared to the open pathway of the human ear, the chameleon analogue is inefficient, losing most of the higher frequencies. While the ear can register sound from 100 to 10,000 cycles per second, it senses between 200 and 600 cycles best. Chameleons don't respond to tones much above middle C. If they listened to music, they would favor works for the tuba. Whatever use they have for sound, it exists in the lower registers.

Chameleons can't hear danger or food approaching, and they can't sniff it out either. Snakes use the Jacobson's organ (also called the vomeronasal organ) to enhance their sense of smell because the chemical receptors in their nostrils are relatively insensitive. The tiny organ sits in the roof of the mouth. When the snake flicks its tongue, it returns with airborne molecules for the chemoreceptors of the organ to assess.

Part of this reptilian sensory apparatus doesn't operate in chameleons; chameleon skulls lack the bone that separates the Jacobson's organ from the nasal cavity. For many years researchers believed they didn't possess the organ, but investigators in this century have found a vestigial organ. In their early embryo stage, chameleons exhibit the balance between the Jacobson's organ and nasal olfactory organs normally seen in reptiles. As the lizards mature inside the eggs, the Jacobson's organ fails to keep pace with the growth of the chemoreceptors in the nostrils. And while the organ is present in adults, it has no function. The principle of ontogeny recapitulating pylogeny suggests chameleons once had functioning and presumably useful Jacobson's organs, but the structure atrophied with disuse as they came to depend on their specialized feeding strategies.

Tongue testing among chameleons remains an enigma. All species, ages and genders of chameleons press a bilobed organ near the front of the tongue against objects for a moment. The organ has no function in feeding. Because chameleons wipe the cloaca on branches after defecating, some researchers speculate that the tongue test may pick up chemical messages.

The chameleon's visual system develops early. Most chameleons possess a pineal eye, also called a parietal or third eye, extruding from the epiphysis of the brain to the center of the forehead. A hole in the skull allows it to sense heat and light, and a layer of skin and connective material covers and protects it. The pineal eye appears to play a role in controlling basking, breeding, egg laying and hibernation. Just as chameleons seem to be abandoning the use of the Jacobson's organ, it's likely the "third eye" will fall into disuse as they depend more and more on vision. Chameleons with body parietal crests covering the eye have already lost use of the pineal eye.

The Jackson's, Johnston's (top) and sail-fin chameleons (below) are among the species with pronounced horns. Like most females, the female Jackson's (following page) has a smaller protuberance.

A chameleon is the most visually reliant of animals. Chameleons communicate through visual cues conveyed by color and posture changes, and they read the cues with their color vision. With the impoverishment of its other senses, the chameleon depends on its eyes to detect rivals, mates, predators and prey. In essence, evolution has restricted the skills open to chameleons for hunting. Unable to hear, smell or run down their prey, they depend completely on their miraculous eyes and tongue.

The chameleon's eyes work like those of no other animal in the world. Only the pupil peers out of a protruding dome of skin, a fused set of eyelids. The chameleon eye contains vastly more cells used for vision than in humans. Each eye covers 180 degrees and operates independent of the other, and when they work together, the creature can judge depth stereoscopically. No other animal has both 3-D vision and the advantage of seeing to the side and behind. How the chameleon's tiny brain can process shifting, complex spatial information is a riddle and one key to its success in the wild. Perhaps abandoning or restricting most of the other senses allowed the chameleon brain to master the complexities of its perceptual system.

Chameleons can hunt and spy predators without moving their heads or bodies. Unless both eyes function optimally, the lizard has difficulty gauging the distance to its prey. When it spots a likely meal, both eyes converge on the target, giving the lizard a silly, cross-eyed look. A chameleon using both eyes hits the target about nine times out of ten. The chameleon starts chewing whether it hits or misses, even if it can still see the prey. One-eyed chameleons can still hunt, although their success rate drops to a little less than two out of three. In a laboratory experiment scientists temporarily blinded a dozen chameleons with adhesive tape over one eye. The first day, none could capture an insect, but by the second day they were hitting over 20% and more than 50% by the fourth day.

After a bit of rocking to enhance stereoscopic vision and confirm range—an inch too short or too long will cause a miss—the chameleon deploys its lightning tongue. Except for its ability to spring more than a body length away, hit a tiny and sometimes moving target and reel it back to the mouth, all in the blink of an eye, a chameleon's tongue differs from a human's only in detail. A "U"-shaped hyoid bone anchors the tongue to the back of the mouth. The same musculature is used to move the tongue in the mouth and swallow. But chameleon evolution has added to the arsenal of lingual tricks.

Since the early 19th century scientists tried to explain how chameleons could move their tongues with blurring speed. The tongue can extend between one and one-and-one-half body lengths with dead-eyed accuracy and blurring speed. A 5½-inch tongue reaches full extension in one-sixteenth of a second, fast enough to pluck a fly from the air. One theory supposed that chameleons instantaneously inflated their hollow tongues with air from their lungs, but no such connection was found. Another postulated that the tongue filled with blood like a high-speed penis. In 1836 the French anatomist Georges-Louis Duvernoy insisted that muscular contractions forced the tongue from the mouth, and all subsequent investigations substantiated his view. But the purpose of the unique structures of chameleon anatomy and the intricate sequence of muscle movements required for them to feed became clear only in the 1930s, when researchers severed tongue muscles to learn which controlled extension and which retracted.

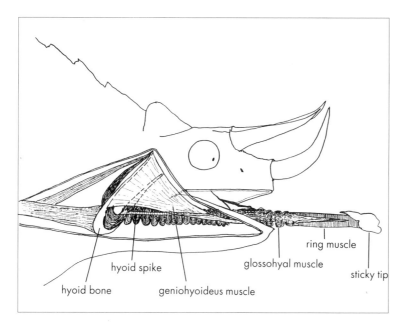

The complex structure of the chameleon's tongue and jaws.

The hollow tongue sheathes over a long, tapering cartilaginous spike called the hyoid horn. The horn attaches to the center of the hyoid bone. The tongue consists of three primary components: the sticky tip, the retractor muscles and the accelerator muscles, musculus accelerator linguae in scientific parlance. When at rest, the whole assembly sits at the bottom of the mouth, the base placed down in the throat behind the head. Before striking, the lizard moves it toward the front of the mouth like a cannon on a sled. Muscles raise the hyoid bone above the lower jaw. After aiming with the entire head, the chameleon is ready to fire.

The accelerator muscles are essentially sphincters. These rings of muscle squeeze against the hyoid horn. Because the horn tapers toward the tip, the muscles drive the entire tongue out of the mouth. Lubricated cavities between the muscles and the bone reduce friction so the tongue can fly with greater speed. The effect is the same as squeezing a watermelon seed to make it fly, except in this case the seed remains stationary and the squeezer is propelled into space.

Chameleon tongues act more like cannonballs than guided missiles in flight. Once the accelerators fire, the only control the lizard can exert is length of strike. A tendon attaches to the tip of the hyoid horn. This and other tendons stop the tongue in flight, thus shielding delicate musculature from the shock.

The tip of the tongue resembles a club. Covered with a sticky saliva, its abrasive surface also grips. High-speed photographs of the tongue in flight reveal a flap of skin trailing the head of the club. The flap wraps partially around the prey on impact. Wet worms or slugs, however, frustrate the system because the saliva won't adhere to their slimy surface.

The retractor (glossohyal) muscles fold around the hyoid horn like a compressed accordion. When the tongue extends, the elastic retractors stretch smoothly to the tip of the horn. Then, after a hit or a miss, the muscle contracts, bringing the rest of the tongue with it. The tongue can pull in about half of the chameleon's body weight. Because speed is less important for reeling in prey than catching it, the retractors don't exhibit the speed of the accelerator muscles. Most of the time the tongue collapses and recoils on the way back, a like a strand of spaghetti being sucked in.

Unlike many reptiles, chameleon chew their food. The eyes resume scanning for danger or more food even as the jaws

As with other chameleons, C. nasutus *uses its protuberance for combat with other males and to recognize others of its species.*

work. But if a chameleon inadvertently captured an inedible object, the tongue pushes the mistake out of the mouth and hunting begins anew.

HORNS

Of all the whimsical ornaments chameleons display, horns and horn-like protuberances are the most spectacular and goofy. What possible use could even the most fearsome-looking appendages serve on a tiny animal incapable of achieving one-quarter mile per hour even when charging in a rage?

Most chameleon horns aren't horns at all. Called rostral protuberances, these scale-covered growths sprout above the nostrils and range in size from unobtrusive knobs to twin crests flaring above the nostrils like the tail fins on a 1950s Buick. Unlike true horns, they are often flexible. *Xenorhinus* rocks through the forests of the Mountains of the Moon in Central Africa sporting a double spatula of scales jutting ahead of his skull, and Madagascar's *Chamaeleo gallus* grows a flexible scale-covered blade as long as its head.

While the distribution of species with rostal protuberances extends from the east coast of Madagascar to the Atlantic coast of Africa, only a minority of African species, such as Jackson's, Johnston's and Fulleborni chameleons, grow true horns with bony cores and keratinized sheaths. The horns are annulated, that is, they grow in rings. In some species the females grow only minimal horns or no horns at all. Male Jackson's chameleons grow three horns, one from the snout (rostral) and two above the eyes (praeorbital), while most females grow a small rostral horn at best, but there's a good deal of variation among the females throughout the Jackson's range. Most chameleons with true horns grow three like the Jackson's, but *quadracornis* flaunts four.

The chameleon's horn appears useful for combat but it's difficult to imagine the sluggish reptiles charging like rhinoceros and inflicting any damage, yet this is what some do. Lumbering toward the enemy with open mouth, the charging lizard lowers his head and rams his victim, which could cripple his enemy if a horn happens to injure a bulging eye. Scientists have witnessed battles such as these among Jackson's and

Johnston's chameleons. Males with larger horns have an advantage because they can strike their opponent before his horn reaches them. Lizards equipped with rostral protuberances push each other like dueling elk but don't inflict permanent injury unless they bite.

Horns and protuberances have other functions too. Closely related species occupying adjacent or overlapping territories recognize members of their own group in part from the presence or absence of protuberances. If the protuberance is removed, neighboring chameleons act confused, unable to decide whether the maimed chameleon deserves a territorial warning. Other theories scientists have proposed for the horns haven't proved valid. One suggested the blades at the end of the snout of *C. nasutus* channeled water away from the nostrils so the animal could breathe during downpours in its rain forest home; but water beads on the animal's hydrophobic skin, so a rain drain isn't necessary. As with other chameleons, *nasutus* uses its protuberance solely for combat and species recognition.

THE LANGUAGE OF COLOR

In Kenya's Lake Nakuru National Park I once asked a ranger where to find chameleons. "It is impossible to find chameleons," he replied.

"You mean there aren't any here?"

"They are here," he assured me. "It's just impossible to find them."

The chameleon's ability to blend into its environment has led to a host of popular myths. Aristotle was the first to send Western science sniffing down the wrong track. Although he correctly surmised that chameleons changed color in response to temperature, he also suggested that they tried to match their hue to their environment, an error that persists in textbooks today. More recently, chameleons were thought to be in peril if placed on plaid cloth, eventually succumbing to the strain of trying to duplicate the pattern. But the true functions of the chameleon's color change are more wonderful than Aristotle's inaccurate observations and the wild speculations of folklorists.

We now understand the mechanics of color change. Special cells called chromatophores, containing red and yellow pigments, lie in two distinct layers just under the transparent outer skin. A stratum reflecting blue and one reflecting white cover the deepest layer, which contains the brown chemical melanin, the substance responsible for tanning in humans. Fibers of melanin rise up through the other layers like an inverted root system. To modify skin color, color cells expand or shrink, mixing brown, red and yellow in different proportions and masking the reflective layers in varying amounts. An angry chameleon sends melanin toward the skin's surface, blocking the white layer and darkening the animal. If yellow cells enlarge over the blue cells, a calm green results. Color change is rapid and results in increased skin temperature.

While researchers believe they can describe the way the skin changes color, the process for triggering a pattern, the link from brain to skin, resists explanation. Some scientists suspect a series of chemical signals prompt the changes, while others believe the evidence points to nervous control. For example, if a chameleon, black with anger, is decapitated, the severed head remains dark while the body becomes pale. This suggests central nervous system control but doesn't preclude actions by hormonal or other systems in concert with nervous activity.

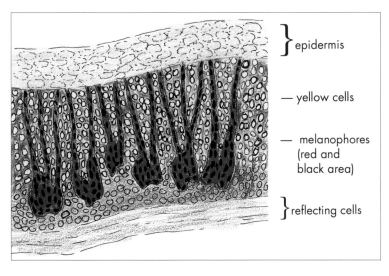

Changes in a chameleon's skin color are caused by the rising of melanin through layers of skin cells containing red and yellow pigment.

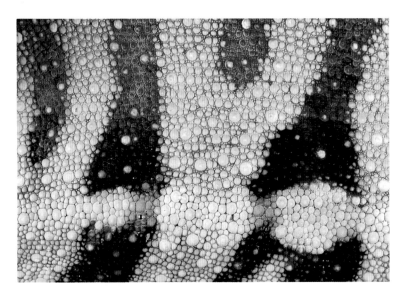

Changes in skin color are affected by mood. Here, C. pardalis *when angered (above) and when calm, several minutes later (below).*

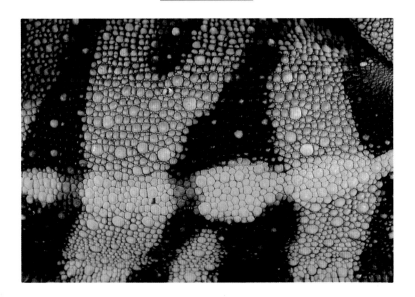

The Jackson's in our house shifted hues for almost any reason, except to match the background. When angry, our Jackson's changed from a uniform pale green to a mottled charcoal or a diamond pattern in less than a minute. One male yellowed his lips to woo his would-be girlfriend. Another came out of surgery completely black; when the vet put him in my wife's hand, he quickly returned to a soft green. But even these displays pale compared to the pyrotechnics of Madagascar's panther chameleon, which can shift from shades of green to lemon and lime daubed with scarlet in moments. *Lambertoni* chameleons change from their usual lime, lemon and turquoise to black and white, flecked with old gold and robin's egg blue. When dying, they darken and sometimes display bright highlights. A dead chameleon looks drab.

Color plays a critical role in the chameleon's social life. Male chameleons generally live alone, guarding their territory jealously. Any intruder merits vigorous countermeasures. For many chameleon species, territorial battles consist of aggressive displays, not physical contests. After spotting a rival, the chameleon turns sideways to the threat, flattens its body, curls its tail and thrusts out its throat. With lungs branching throughout their body, they puff themselves up, thus presenting a literally inflated image. For those species that have them, males raise flaps behind their helmeted head. *Chamaeleo cucullatus* raises the flap opposite his opponent, then turns toward him. From the opponent's point of view, he now has a terrifyingly large head. *Dilepis,* the African common chameleon, wiggles both flaps simultaneously. *Carpenteri,* a grotesque creature from the Mountains of the Moon, depends on a high spatulate casque to persuade others to abandon hope.

Males of all species substitute a pugnacious pattern of colors intended to intimidate opponents for those adopted on an uneventful day. Both contenders understand the symbolism. Finally, they open their mouths, exposing the contrasting colors of their mucus membranes, often accompanied by a choreography of swaying and bobbing punctuated by soft hisses. In most species, this signals the end of the conflict as one usually concedes aesthetic defeat, changes to the color of an inoffensive juvenile and slinks away. If the intruder fails to bolt after confronted by the full arsenal of threats, the defender will charge. This usually decides the contest, but several of the larger varieties will run down the offender and inflict real damage, sometimes killing him with savage bites.

The females of most species usually don't engage in threat behavior when they encounter other females, and they don't confine themselves to one small area. A female passes through successive male territories, which increases the chances for copulation and reduces the chances of inbreeding. Females likely led the dispersal of chameleons across Africa into Europe, the Middle East and India.

Thus, color changes are not used as a disguise, but make the chameleon more conspicuous because the intent is not to hide but to communicate. The study of chameleon semantics began in the 1970s when Steven Parcher, a researcher from Johns Hopkins University, spent nine months in Madagascar's eastern rain forest studying six interacting species. Since chameleons prefer a solitary life and seldom mingle, the odds of observing many confrontations was low. To increase the number of encounters, he captured specimens of the same species and thrust them together in the bush. After careful observation, he discovered that specific pattern and color combinations corresponded to threats or courtship maneuvers. The color and pattern code differed for each variety of chameleon.

Color plays a role in courtship for many animals, including reptiles. Instead of fanning tail feathers or wearing a perpetual bright crest, chameleons dress for each occasion. When a male locates a sexually mature female, he adopts his flashiest colors and bobs his head in a special pattern. The colors and head bobbing choreography differ among species, but all exhibit some variation. Temperature determines the speed of head-jerking—the warmer, the faster. Head-jerking and other display attributes may be used to define species someday, but scientists have charted few displays and their taxonomic potential remains untapped.

After catching sight of a female, the diminutive *nasutus* chameleon abandons his usual brown coloration for purple banded with light blue. His eyelids become yellow and a patch of light green appears behind each eye. The male *brevicornis*, also usually predominantly brown, adds a deep red or maroon to his occipital lobes and rostral appendix. His eyelids turn orange or yellow and dark patterns mark his flanks. The giant Parson's merely intensifies its normal dull green, adding a light green patch behind the eye. All three species accompany courtship color change with lateral flattening and head jerks.

To discover the importance of color versus choreographed anatomical displays in courtship, Parcher marked the males with a felt-tip pen to look like females. He showed wild chameleons plastic chameleon models that emphasized individual

As with some other species, C. brevicornis *puffs up his gular crest and raises his occipital lobes in threat displays.*

characteristics, such as occipital lobes or rostral formations. Most of the time the wild lizards either ignored the experiment or reacted as if the markings did not exist. Out of 100 experiments only two males fell for the ruse and tried to mount a painted male. Parcher also stained females to mask their threat colors during threat displays. He found that males didn't respond to females when they couldn't "read" female threat colors.

Parcher concluded that chameleons use color change for species and gender recognition. Since similar species share habitat, to confirm that a female is of the correct species, a male adopts courting colors and behaviors. The female responds to his overtures with her own repertoire of threats and color change. If her response confirms that she belongs to his species, the male will continue his display and warily approach. A male may not recognize a female of his own species until she threatens him.

Like other chameleons, the male C. brevicornis *changes from a dull brown to more colorful hues to attract a female's attention.*

For many chameleon species the term "courtship" rings false. These males don't persuade females by staging impressive displays or defeating rival males. Instead, they rush females and mount them before they can escape. The female struggles and continues her threat display throughout. Copulation begins after the male has a firm grip on the female's back. He then extrudes his hemipenes and inserts one into her cloaca. Because the sperm travels slowly on the outside of the hemipenis, copulation requires fifteen minutes or more to complete. The lizards sit motionless, looking all around. During the act, our male Jackson's rolled his eyes like Groucho Marx delivering a double entendre.

If approached too closely by a male, the female will attack. During courtship, females never approach the male except to attack him and drive him away. These confrontations rarely end in copulation. Frustrated in his quest for a romantic assignation, the male often loses interest after several rejections and seeks another mate.

GROWING UP

Like most reptiles, most chameleon lay eggs. A few days before laying her eggs, the female climbs down to dig a nest in the earth. For many species, egg laying time comes when the earth is soft from rain. Because eggs need a moist environment, the mother will dig until she finds damp soil, even in a desert.

A chameleon digs as slowly as she walks. Often she digs for days, returning to the safety of the branches to sleep. When working on the nest she's vulnerable—conspicuous, preoccupied and slow. If a predator stumbles upon her, she has no defense except bluffing or playing dead.

When the nest is deep enough, usually deeper than her length from tip to tail, she deposits from 30 to 50 eggs. After adding the last egg to the clutch, she fills the hole with her customary deliberation and tamps the ground to restore its original undisturbed appearance. With the hole concealed, she climbs back to the branches, never to return. In captivity, females often die from the stress of egg laying, but in the wild they lay several clutches a year without undue strain.

The embryonic chameleons grow under the surface for weeks or months. The leathery shell absorbs water throughout the incubation period. Nobody knows what triggers hatching, although swings in temperature, humidity and rainfall seem likely.

When conditions are right, the babies emerge. They struggle free of the egg and tunnel to the surface. Upon arriving, they hustle to a nearby bush and climb to relative safety. At this point in their development, their color usually matches the brown of bark and branches, concealing them from predators and potential meals. The young of some species, however, display bright colors, which may consign them to a predator's belly in short order. The female Parson's starts life the color of a ripe persimmon. Whatever survival value bright color affords is unknown.

Even with their protective coloration, the young lizards may find safety elusive. At birth they're no larger than a fingernail. All the carnivores feared by their elders would like to munch a baby chameleon as well, and a host of meat eaters intimidated by adults will feast on the tiny reptiles. Spiders and mantises have no trouble subduing and devouring them, and even a group of ants can sting a baby with their poisonous jaws and eat it. Some never have a chance to encounter a predator; they fall victim to animals who sniff out the nest and dig up the eggs.

Babies have even fewer defenses than adults. They try to bluff, puffing out their throats and turning sideways to the threat, displaying their scariest colors. When this fails, they jump, or rather fall deliberately, to the ground. Sometimes predators won't bother to pursue.

Some chameleon species increase the odds of survival by eliminating the months of burial in the nest and the race to the bushes. Unlike their oviparous, or egg laying, cousins, these mothers give live birth. Unlike mammals, chameleons are ovoviviparous instead of viviparous. The embryos develop within eggs inside the mother. Nutrients in the egg sustain them as they grow and the mother becomes a "mobile nest." Montane species especially tend to be ovoviviparous. The *Bradypodion,* or *pumilus,* group gives live birth as well. No theory satisfactorily explains why some species adopted live birth while their neighbors continued to dig nests.

Among the live-bearing species, the egg at birth consists of a thin gooey membrane. The female presses her cloaca against the branch as each egg emerges so that it sticks. Then, she moves a bit and deposits another. Within minutes the babies

Males and females of the same species can differ markedly in color,
as is the case with these male and female pardalis.

break free. Sometimes the egg fails to adhere and falls to the ground, tearing on impact. Unhurt, the baby marches to a bush and climbs away from danger.

From the first, baby chameleons walk and climb with assurance, on the lookout for their first meal. When a small insect comes into view, the slender tongue darts with near-perfect accuracy. If they cross paths with another chameleon of their species, they communicate as well as adults.

If they survive the rigors of childhood, they may live a decade or more. No one knows for sure the life span of chameleons in the wild. Captive Jackson's have lived almost 10 years in ideal captive conditions, but that figure may not apply to wild individuals or members of other species.

ENEMIES

When camouflage and bluff fail to deter a predator, a chameleon is nearly helpless. Almost any carnivore smaller than a lion or larger than a gerbil considers the chameleon edible. Once it's spotted there is no escape. As a last resort some species feign death, flopping on their sides, letting their tongue loll, and shifting to their drabbest colors. This tactic works against animals that disdain carrion.

Rats and shrews dine on smaller chameleons, and the tiny nasutus, the smallest chameleon at about two grams, occasionally serves as dinner for the praying mantis and the orb weaving spider. Inactive at night, chameleons are easy prey for nocturnal animals prowling the branches, including birds and snakes. The venomous boomslang snake is a primary predator of Jackson's chameleons. Some species save themselves from nocturnal predation with a drop reflex. If a vibration disturbs the branch where they sleep, feet and tail relax, and the chameleon drops to the ground.

More chameleons find their way into the stomachs of birds than the insides of any other group of predators. Hawks, kites and cuckoos pluck them from branches, and owls nab them wherever they hide. Shrikes impale them on thorns and eat them at their convenience. Thus, chameleons must pay attention to the skies, keeping one eye on passing airplanes just to be sure.

However voracious, predators never comprise a threat to the existence of an entire population of chameleons in any area. Their birth rate and effectiveness at hiding sustain their numbers despite the best efforts of birds and boomslangs. But in many parts of Africa and in all of Madagascar, man has disturbed the balance and threatens to wipe many species out of existence. Chameleons thrive in circumscribed niches. They've learned to hid in particular plants, and to eat the insects the ecosystem supports. The loss of a single type of plant could doom a highly specialized lizard, and when a forest falls to accommodate agriculture, such lizards have no way to adapt quickly.

Island species are especially vulnerable. Because islands evince less biodiversity, any changes induce profound effects. For example, on the Pacific island of Guam an imported tree snake drove endemic birds to extinction. They had developed no strategies against a predator that could climb to their nests. The vulnerability of island species was demonstrated again when a shift in Pacific Ocean currents, El Niño, nearly annihilated the population of Galapagos marine iguanas in the 1980s. Unfortunately, almost half of all chameleon species live on islands: Madagascar, Sri Lanka and smaller islands in the Indian Ocean.

All these islands, but especially Madagascar, are under ecological assault. Madagascar has been called the greatest ecological disaster in history. In an effort to keep pace with an exploding population, the populace has intensified traditional slash and burn farming techniques. Charcoal is considered a cash crop; farmers will burn a teak tree for two bags of charcoal worth just over a dollar. As a result, only a fraction of the island's forests remain. Consequent erosion scars the landscape, and topsoil built over millions of years washes into the sea. In the rainy season the rivers run red, choked with minerals. Astronauts say the island looks like it's bleeding. The populace is flushing its future down the rivers, and the wildlife is likely to go with it.

Concurrently, the chameleon population dwindles in the remaining habitat as impoverished people make a pittance by supplying the pet trade. They fill sacks with these profoundly anti-social reptiles, often breaking their legs and feet as they pull them off the branches. Few survive transport to Europe or

Though the baby Parson's chameleon (top) is a bright orange color, the young of most other species, like the baby C. pardalis (below), are duller than their parents.

Along with other animals, chameleon species in Madagascar are threatened with habitat loss. Some colorful Madagascar species include C. lateralis *and* C. pardalis.

the United States, and those that arrive in a pet store usually die in a few weeks from accumulated stress.

Madagascar and other nations with chameleon populations are signatories of the C.I.T.E.S. treaty, an international agreement regulating the traffic in threatened and endangered animals. While in theory the treaty limits damage to wild populations from the pet trade, traders often ignore its provisions, sneaking shipments out of Madagascar and Africa with the aid of a few trifling bribes. Even the environmental laws within each country receive scant notice. Madagascar forbids the export of wild-caught chameleons, but so-called farms, ostensibly raising captive-bred reptiles, are often nothing more than holding cells for wild-caught animals.

The only legitimate argument for exporting captured chameleons is to embark on bona fide captive breeding programs. Zoos, herpetologists and hobbyists have tried with varying success.

Captive populations may not save species over the long term. Scientists studying cheetahs noticed an unusual lack of genetic diversity. In a genetically diverse population some individuals would possess resistant immune systems. Many may have impoverished their gene pool by capturing the largest and strongest cats to grace the royal courts of Europe and Asia. Centuries of human predation, in the service of human vanity, pauperized the remaining population as the weakest cats propagated. A disease attacking a genetic weakness could wipe out the remaining wild cheetahs. The limited genetic diversity of chameleons in captivity puts them at risk, too.

FOUR REPRESENTATIVE CHAMELEONS

In the preceding chapter we've looked at the range of chameleon survival strategies, both structural and behavioral. Each species solves the problems posed by its environment differently, and since chameleons live in habitats with contradictory demands, from rain forest to desert, from oven-like heat to mountain chill, each species has found unique yet effective ways to deal with the challenges of its home. In the profiles below we will look at the solutions adopted by particular species of chameleon from the desert, the mountains and the coastal jungle, and at the fascinating African dwarf chameleon.

A DESERT CHAMELEON:
CHAMAELEO NAMAQUENSIS

The Namaqua chameleon acts like none of its *Chamaeleo* cousins. As an adult it is wholly terrestrial. In adapting to life on the ground, it depends on speed as well as stealth to evade predators unlike its slow relatives. Considering its anomalous behavior and structure, the Namaqua belongs on the fringes of the genus.

In 1838 an observer wrote, "When [approached] these cameleons . . . open their mouths . . . and hissed like angry snakes, whilst a bag under their mouths swelled to a great size, which, with their dark, blotched bodies, gave them a hideous appearance. They run fast, and are accounted to be poisonous to the natives."

The Namaqua lives in semi-arid and desert regions on the Atlantic coast of southern Africa, including the Namib Desert, one of the driest places on Earth. Once considered an isolated species, it is now seen as a close relative of the common chameleon, *Chamaeleo chamaeleon*, the other desert dweller in the genus. Like *C. chamaeleon*, *C. namaquensis* features homogeneous squamation, with scales sometimes arranged in rosette-shaped groups, and its skull lacks occipital lobes. The central parietal crest is elevated in the back and rises higher than the lateral crest. It grows to 10 inches in length.

The Namaqua chameleon can achieve about three miles per hour and perform "high-speed" evasive maneuvers. Unlike every other chameleon, it can run from danger. Its staple diet consists of beetles supplemented by smaller snakes, lizards and geckos, although one was seen to eat a snake twice its length. In turn, cobras, vipers and monitor lizards hunt the Namaqua.

Thermoregulation

Animals living amid the Namib dunes endure wild temperature swings. Chilling morning fog near the coast drives temperatures to near freezing. When the sun burns through, the walls of sand, some 600 feet high, act as a reflector oven, and the mercury climbs to 150° F at ground level. Cold-blooded animals, whose internal temperatures vary with the temperature of the air, need to conserve or dissipate heat to regulate their own temperature and survive. The Namaqua chameleon employs a host of tactics to maintain a comfortable core temperature between 60° F and 105° F, which is cool for a desert species. If body temperature passes 105° F, the lizard looks for shade, eyes bulging and mouth agape. Mouth gaping is the last gasp tactic for animals in a dry environment: the evaporation of moisture in the mouth cools, but can also desiccate the animal; for some reason, Namaqua chameleons suffer little moisture loss through this tactic.

In the cool of the morning, Namaquas press their bellies against the ground, angling themselves so one side, colored dark purple or black to soak up warmth, basks in the sun. The air sac under the throat inflates to capture heat. Valves in the lungs segregate, warming the air circulating during respiration in special compartments. Sacs surrounding the brain sustain an optimal temperature. Using the same principle as the down jacket, the lizard wraps itself in insulating air pockets under its skin.

After warming the lungs, the Namaqua compresses its body to 30% of normal width and aligns itself perpendicular to the sun. The side facing the sun stays dark while the other side lightens. After a few minutes, the animal turns the other side to the rays and reverses its coloration. On windy days Namaquas plough a shallow two-way groove in the ground to reduce heat loss from convection. Burrowing blocks the breeze and reduces wind chill. Until they absorb sufficient heat, they remain motionless except to eat, court or defend territory.

During warming, the black chameleon is a sitting duck. Usually, the chameleon's skin matches its environment. The Namaqua adopts a light pink to match the dunes of the interior and the Namaquas living on the Atlantic coast are sulphur yellow blotched with brown and brick to blend with the gray-white sand. A passing bird of prey can easily spot a black lizard against the pale ground, however. The faster the lizard reaches operating temperature, the better its chances of survival.

Once warmed, the chameleon maintains a narrow range of temperature. As heat builds, the side facing the sun pales while the skin in shade adopts patterns. In the cool of late afternoon, the Namaqua ploughs a deeper groove (6 inches) to snatch the last bit of warmth. (At the end of the day, heat has penetrated deeper into the ground than in the morning.) After absorbing the last few calories, the reptile decamps to a crevice or burrow where wind, fog and enemies can't disturb it.

Namaquas and the Mediterranean common chameleon are the only members of their genus known to dig for shelter. They prefer to dig in a root system, which binds the soil and prevents cave-ins. If a handy rodent hole presents itself, they use it. If no shelter is available, they camp in the open, positioning themselves in the shade of the setting sun so the first rays of dawn will warm them.

Scientists probing thermoregulatory mechanisms have invented surprising ways to test reptilian response to temperature change. They found that lizards wearing cloth coats don't warm as fast as lizards au naturel. Coats do help retain heat, however. By injecting water just below the skin, to determine how effectively the Namaquas absorb or dissipate heat, researchers have shown that the circulatory system plays a large role in temperature control. The animal directs blood flow to the skin to affect body temperature, an ability scientists call peripheral dermal vasomotor control. Blood vessels constrict near the skin to prevent heat loss when it's cold or while the animal sleeps. The vessels dilate and blood flows freely during basking to transfer heat rapidly.

The three-chambered reptile heart can also vary blood flow to different areas of the body. In the Namaqua, warmer, more oxygenated blood moves to the brain and other vital organs first. Chameleons possess a carotid body, a chemoreceptor in the carotid arteries (which feed the brain) that responds to changes in oxygen levels in the blood, thus contributing to control of respiration and delivery of warm, oxygenated blood to critical organs. The rear of the animal tolerates reduced oxygen without damage for a time, allowing the carotid body to divert blood to vital organs without harming the animal. Once the essential organs reach optimal temperature, the circulatory system equalizes, and the rear of the animal receives its share of warmth and oxygen.

Hunting and Defense

While Namaquas usually hunt in conventional chameleon fashion, using stealth and tongue, they sometimes chase beetles or small lizards and grab them with their jaws. If a small creature hides under a rock or in a bush, to flush it out the chameleon turns over the stones or shakes the brush where the tracks disappear. When aggressive tactics fail, the chameleon waits in ambush for the creature to appear.

On the Namib, however, there's a fine line between predator and prey, and many of the creatures the Namaqua hunts

C. namaquensis *survives in a harsh desert climate.*

can harm or kill it. The lizard learns to strike a viper in the head with its tongue and crush its skull before it can bite. The tongue can also be used to strike wasps on the lower abdomen and scorpions just below the stinger, using a different strategy for each hazardous species. Once the prey is in the mouth, the chameleon chews off the dangerous part and spits out the animal. After examining it to confirm that the dangerous part has been successfully separated from the rest of the animal, the chameleon swallows it. Sometimes the chameleon chews, spits and examines the prey several times before concluding the threat is gone. In the case of a large scorpion, the chameleon removes the claws after snipping the stinger, before dining at leisure. Young lizards carelessly go after dangerous prey without precautions. After receiving injuries, they develop adult strategies for handling dangerous prey. Both young and old eat until the stomach is full.

Namaquas are gourmands. Living along the beach, they patrol the shore at low tide, sprayed by nearby surf, feeding on arthropods and flying insects. Salt ingested with marine prey is excreted through the nostrils and scraped away with the claws or by rubbing the nose against the ground. The chameleons supplement their diet with plants, presumably for both nutrients and water. When lucky, they nab small birds. They even eat their own shed skin.

In the almost rainless Namib, the lizards rely on frequent fogs for water. They snag droplets from plants with their tongues, lap moisture from rocks or lick condensation running down their faces. Even on clear days, enough dew condenses for the lizards to drink in the morning and at dusk. Moisture in their prey helps slake their thirst, too. Unlike many desert species, they store little water in their bodies; however, the cloaca reabsorbs water before excretion.

C. namaquensis doesn't behave toward threats with the resignation found in other chameleon species and is a fighter if pressed. It will try to run when caught away from cover, but if you encounter one motionless, it freezes. While it tracks you with its eyes, the body remains stationary and the color pale. You can pass your hand in front of the face or bridge the body with your fingers without eliciting a response, but any contact throws the lizard into a fury, hissing and growling with jaws agape, displaying a yellow-orange mouth. Standing tall and compressed, it turns black and puffs out the throat, revealing the yellow and rust of interstitial skin. Back away and it switches to pale colors and runs in an eccentric path to escape. If you don't back off, the chameleon will charge. If forced to bite, it chomps hard and refuses to let go, twisting and jerking to create maximum damage.

When Namaquas meet, they fight over territory. Warnings and displays precede combat. Stiff-legged and hissing, they compress laterally and turn black. With throat engorged and exposing bright interstitial skin, they weave the front of their bodies left to right and up and down, the defender executing a tightly choreographed series of head bobs. Each bob describes a sideways "S," the head beginning and ending each bob on the right. Five quick traversals or the "S" constitute a set and require three seconds to perform. After a one-second rest, the reptile repeats the set once or twice. If the transgressor doesn't take the hint, the defender will charge. Namaquas don't have a submissive color and posture—they run or fight—and because of their powerful jaws, battles result in serious injury or death.

After warming in the morning, Namaquas patrol the outer limits of their territory like soldiers guarding a hostile frontier. Borders follow high ground, and territories don't overlap. If they spot another chameleon outside their territory, they initiate displays, but only trespassing sparks a fight. As the day progresses, the patrol spirals toward the center of the territory, where the lizard sleeps. Female territories usually border male's. Sexual encounters spring from border incidents, and after mating, the trespasser is evicted.

Courtship

Courtship occurs year 'round, except from April through July. During courtship, both sexes adopt mottled patterns. The male "dances" around the female, who maintains a threat posture or merely ignores his efforts throughout. He weaves slowly side to side with is entire body while his head describes the lazy "S" of territorial disputes. If she seems receptive, i.e., if she doesn't run or attack, he jerks his head quickly, stands taller, compresses more tightly and raises his tail high. The female may pretend to bite but in fact just nudges her mate. Both parties open their mouths, hissing, weaving, lunging and whipping their tails. Copulation lasts for five to 15 minutes and may be repeated several times a day and several times per week. An unwilling female is dangerous to approach. Female Namaquas are larger than males, and unwanted attentions lead to attacks that often disable or kill the male.

Namaquas lay their eggs in nests constructed near the crests of small dunes or at the windward base of larger ones in their territory. Sometimes the nest is an extension of the female's burrow, which may allow her to protect the eggs from predators. A week before laying, she digs exploratory holes before committing to a site. She tunnels through dry sand, past a moist layer, and excavates a chamber in the dry sand below. She digs with her eyes closed, using her head as a battering ram. She braces herself with one forefoot and one rear, using the other two to throw sand behind her. When the pile behind her grows, she backs out of the tunnel and flicks sand into a pile of trails that eventually reaches over three feet high. She climbs to the top and shakes the sand from her head. After opening her eyes, she returns to the tunnel to continue her work. Nest digging takes from eight to 10 hours.

The female lays her eggs upon completion of the nest. She lays six to eight eggs, pauses to cover them with sand, and deposits another layer. A clutch may consist of six to 22 eggs. She has two or three clutches each year.

After three to four months of incubation, the eggs hatch in late evening and into the night. The babies disperse immediately and climb trees for safety. When they get larger, as they try to climb their favorite grasses, the plants collapse under the weight and the discouraged youngsters abandon climbing for good. The young have no territories and the adults don't bother them. The Namib provides plenty of food for all. They reach maturity in 150 to 210 days. Females mature faster than males.

It is ironic that we know more about the behavior of Namaquas than that of almost any other chameleon, hidden as they are among the giant dunes of one of the world's great deserts, an empty African expanse where less than a million people live in an area larger than Oregon. The common chameleon enjoying the sun on the Mediterranean coast is more of an enigma.

THE JUNGLE PANTHER:
CHAMAELEO PARDALIS

Even at the highest speeds achievable on the roads of north-western Madagascar—about 30 miles an hour—you can see flashes of red and yellow in the bushes. Chameleon hunting in the wild usually consists of staring at a patch of brush until a chameleon appears from the background, like a figure in an Escher print. But the gaudy *Chamaeleo pardalis*, called the panther chameleon, splashes bright tints against the green as if unconcerned with camouflage. The road from Diégo-Suarez at the island's northern tip to Ambanja is a rutted strip of dirt winding through wet farmland and secondary forest. We saw half a dozen "drive-by" panthers in one day, sunning in the bushes or crossing the road, which we dubbed the Pardalis Highway.

The male *pardalis* can grow to over a foot in length. Scale crests bristle along its stomach, neck and spine. A strong parietal crest bisects the casque rising behind the forehead, and the two lateral ridges run into two small rostral protuberances, called canthi rostrales, at the end of their snout. The sides of the *pardalis* are stippled with scales of varying sizes and colors. When unthreatened, most of their bodies are shades of dark green with a pale robin's egg blue band traversing each side. When aroused by a rival or a prospective mate, brilliant yellows and reds supplant the greens.

Female panthers lack rostral protuberances; otherwise they resemble scaled-down males but with different colors. Before reaching sexual maturity, females are gray-brown, but when ready to reproduce, they advertise their availability by adopting a uniform salmon orange. After mating the female darkens to black highlighted with orange. Any male who fails to read this color's message—"stay away, I'm pregnant"—will be treated to hissing, mouth-gaping and attack. After laying her eggs, the female returns to bright salmon, ready for breeding once more.

On opposite page:
C. pardalis, *the jungle panther, is one of the most spectacular of chameleon species.*

Panthers live along the east and northern coasts of Madagascar. Along with the ubiquitous *lateralis, pardalis* is the most common and conspicuous chameleon found in resort areas such as Nosy Be. Their habitat is green, hot and humid. Although they live in areas with relatively dense human populations, they don't appear as threatened as other less adaptable species. *Pardalis* are content to hunt for bugs while climbing on fragrant ylang ylang trees or lurking among the rice fields.

Over the centuries panthers colonized many outlying islands. Any day on Nosy Be ("nosy" means island and "be" means big), you'll see several panthers going about their business, and even on minute Nosy Tanikley, a few acres of earth between Nosy Be and the main island, a small population cruises the trees. It's possible to imagine individuals rafting on floating logs to the islands, but they probably hitched a ride on a native's boat. Certainly, only sailing ships could have transported pioneering panthers, either as pets or stowaways, to distant islands such as Réunion, hundreds of miles from Madagascar's shores.

Territoriality

Pardalis are one of the most hostile and territorial chameleons, which explains their common name, the panther chameleon. When one male spies another, he activates his border defenses. First he inflates the lung tissue that webs through his body to swell to his most imposing size. At the same time he angles his body so his swollen flank faces the enemy. With nearly equal speed angry reds and yellows wash over his normal cool green colors.

His opponent responds with the same tactics. The two puffed-up reptiles eye each other for a time before the more aggressive combatant escalates by opening his mouth to expose the dread mucus membranes. This is enough to cow a timid panther, but a macho male will remain unimpressed and undeterred.

Throughout this choreography both lizards move closer. If neither party yields, combat is inevitable. Unlike many chameleons panther often fight to the death. Usually the first to charge prevails, probably from aggression alone since there is neither surprise nor speed to give him an advantage. In most cases, a panther responds to a charge by fleeing or even dropping to

A male pardalis *threatens his reflection in a mirror.*

The immature female pardalis *is a duller brownish color.*

the earth, but if fighting ensues, one will grab the other and bite fiercely, tearing flesh and crushing bones. Eventually the victor releases his victim, but the weakened animal faces a slow death.

Mating

Panther romance displays similar savagery. The males dispense with persuasion and shy approaches, preferring to chase, seize and mate with protesting females. In captivity males must live apart from females; otherwise, the females would suffer from constant harassment.

The females lay a clutch of eggs soon after mating. The mother descends and burrows deep in the ground, digging like an Airedale terrier to a depth greater than the length of her body. Preparing a suitable room takes at least a day. After laying her eggs, usually from 30 to 50, she fills the tunnel and taps the ground flat with her feet. All this activity occurs in broad daylight on the ground, where all chameleon camouflage arts serve no purpose. Laying eggs is a hazardous enterprise the females endure several times a year. The first hatching often doesn't occur for 240 days, and the last lizard doesn't claw his way free for another seven weeks. For some reason, eggs laid in the wild hatch over the course of a few months, perhaps responding to alterations in humidity or other atmospheric effects. The babies hunt from the moment they emerge, all weapons systems operating at 100% efficiency.

When I recently visited a reptile nursery operated by Ron and Marilyn Tremper in Fresno, California, some *pardalis* eggs had recently hatched. Twenty babies, each only an inch or two long, cruised in a cage. In separate enclosures the adults spotted us and drew to attention, ready to fight, warning us to keep our distance by opening their jaws, expanding their throats and darkening their hue. "We have to keep the adults apart," Marilyn explained. "If they even see one another, they threaten and bluster all day. The stress isn't good for them. And the males won't leave the females alone for a minute. They're pretty rough."

As she spoke, she fed the babies, picking infant mealworms from a cup with tweezers and dropping them into the cage. The tiny lizards approached the worms with no hint of stealth, steadied themselves by gripping branches with their tails, aimed at their prey with the distinctive cross-eyed stare, and fired unerringly. "This takes a long time," Marilyn allowed, as 40 eye turrets scanned the cage for food.

Few chameleons do well in captivity, but panthers do better than most. If the importer medicates them for parasitic infestation in Madagascar, ships them swiftly and re-medicates them upon arrival, they have a high survival rate, though gravid females, already weakened by parasites and the rigors of transport, usually die from the added stress of egg laying. Captive breeding programs, like the one run by the Trempers, have succeeded in propagating several generations, and the panthers seem to thrive in terraria. It's possible that a pet trade in captive-born panthers could not only reduce demand for imported chameleons, many of which die en route, but also provide a safety net for this species, as Madagascar undergoes ecological ruin.

Myths

The concept of "fady" rules the people of Madagascar. These taboos, dictated by the dead, vary from tribe to tribe, town to town and family to family. In the south it's fady for a boy to step over the mat of his sister or for a childless woman to enter the house of a pregnant woman. Everywhere on the island a web of fady protects reptiles. It is fady to eat them in a land where butterflies and mouse lemurs with less meat than a frog supplement the diet, and in the north snakes, while feared, are considered symbols of truth and left undisturbed.

A host of superstitions thus protect the panthers. Not only is eating them proscribed, merely touching them provokes horror. Women never handle them, and if a man comes in contact with a chameleon, his wife won't let him touch her for three days. Killing one, even accidentally, brings bad luck on the head of the killer. Taxi drivers who think nothing of hitting a chicken or a dog swerve wildly to avoid a panther. Sometimes a panther halts traffic on the resort island of Nosy Be as it crosses the road with unhurried deliberation.

The island's people believe the panthers commit suicide when food becomes scarce. They report seeing emaciated chameleons climbing to the top of a high tree, letting go with their feet so they dangle by the tip of their tail, and dropping head first to their death. They also believe chameleons are poisonous.

Enrico Cimador, a young Italian naturalist, devoted two years to studying Nosy Be's Lokobe Reserve. He noticed that his cats lost fur in clumps after eating a chameleon so the poison tale seemed well-founded, but he doubted the suicide story until one event changed his mind. "It was the dry season and insects were in short supply," he recounts. "All the *pardalis* were skinny. I spotted one hanging by his tail just as the Malagasy described. He released his grip and fell on his head. I later saw the same behavior several times." Herpetologist Ron Tremper remains skeptical. "I've seen the same thing, but I think a less exotic explanation fits the facts. When food dwindles, the *pardalis* tend to stay high in the trees. This causes an increase in chance encounters, which

A confrontation between two male pardalis *over territory. Angry reds and yellows replace the cooler green colors of the defender's skin.*

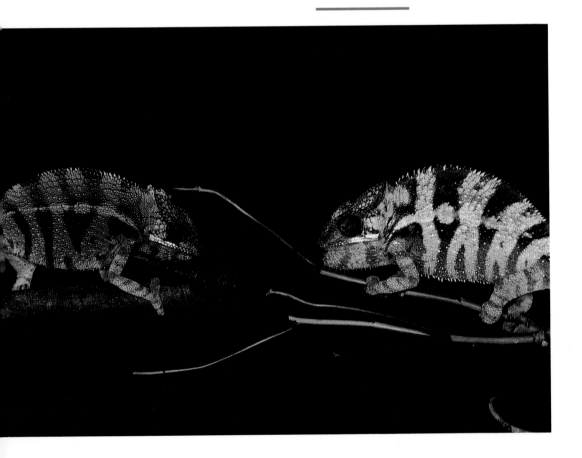

A young pardalis *in sleep colors (above) and normal colors (below).*

result in one fleeing. Panicked *pardalis* get themselves in a bad situation and fall."

The myth of the "chameleon banana" also arose from suspect observation. The "chameleon banana" is the lantana plant, an imported species. Nosy Be's residents gave a flowering bush the name after noticing that *pardalis* often lurked among the blossoms. The locals claim the lizards eat berries the plant produces. It's unlikely the reptiles respond so voraciously to a non-native plant; it's more likely they favor the bush because the flowers attract insects. It's possible the natives saw them reel in a berry after an errant tongue missed an insect, but more observation, not hearsay, is needed to substantiate panther experiments in vegetarianism.

HIGH-ALTITUDE REPTILES: *CHAMAELEO HOEHNELII*

High on the slopes of Mt. Kenya cold rain falls on hardwood forests interlaced with vines and draped in moss. Bamboo bristles upward in open areas, crackling like paper kites when the winds blow up from the savannah. Adventurous elephants and buffalo explore the forest floor and monkeys chatter above. Amid the foliage perch tiny, jewel-like, casque-headed chameleons, *Chamaeleo hoehnelii*.

This species lives in an environment that would kill most chameleons overnight. Temperatures drop near freezing frequently, and witnesses have seen *hoehnelii* walking along a snow covered branch. They are masters of thermoregulation, able to conserve heat during the chilly nights and then warm themselves from sunlight filtered through the clouds at sunrise.

The casque-headed chameleons earned their moniker from the helmet that curves from their eyes to the back of their neck like a medieval sallet. A fringe of skin-flaps under their neck, a gular crest, gives them a comical bearded look. Males and females differ in color and posture. Females remain a uniform green, growing lighter or darker depending on light intensity. Males proclaim every change in mood or status by flying new colors. When a male dominates his territories, his colors brighten, yellow green on his back with a reddish crest and turquoise on his chest and stomach. Non-breeding young males display two yellow lines down their sides over a gray-green or gray-brown background. Sexually mature males prevented from mating by the presence of a dominant male sulk, displaying a dusky green.

Males tend to rest on branches with their bodies outstretched while females curl into a hunched position. Mature males sport a broad casque and prominent scales running down the spine. In general, females have a tapering, narrow-based casque and a more modest dorsal crest, but a minority grow casques and crests almost as large as the males'. Postural and morphological differences are useful for sex recognition when color isn't decisive.

Combat

Unlike fighting panther chameleons, male *hoehnelii* engage in a largely harmless ritual. A fight begins when one male strays into the territory of another during mating season. Head bobbing initiates the conflict. Their yellow and turquoise coloration becomes more vibrant, they flatten their bodies laterally, inflate their gular pouches and turn sideways to each other to present the largest profile. Sometimes this posturing persuades one to abandon the fight and flee, but if posing doesn't decide the issue, the gladiators further inflate and brighten. They slowly approach each other, pausing from time to time to regain maximum inflation and to hiss. Sometimes they suspend the charge to rear up on their hind legs. They sway back and forth on the branches, their mouth gaping to reveal the mucus membranes.

When the lizards get closer, one will try to bite the flattened side of the other. Because the flank is smooth and the jaws approach at a right angle, the teeth can't take hold and the jaws snap without effect. The combatants continue to move in a circle trying to get in position for right angle bites. Occasionally a leg may sustain a bite, but they never go for the throat.

Eventually, one chameleon gives up, adopting submissive, drab juvenile colors and slinking away. If pursued, he falls to

On following page:
C. hoehnelii, *the tiny high-casque chameleon.*

the ground to escape. As soon as the winner is out of eyeshot, the loser resumes his usual bright colors. The victor enhances his already radiant tints and struts away in triumph. When equally matched *hoehnelii* males fight, the intruder loses, but a larger male may take over a territory after chasing away a smaller rival.

In areas of high chameleon population density where encounters and conflicts occur regularly, a pecking order develops. The dominant male maintains his position by display alone after defeating the rival once. Even immature males who wander into the stronger male's territory merit attack. He immediately charges, mouth gaping, prompting an instantaneous disorderly retreat.

Female casque-headed chameleons aggressively try to avoid contact with other chameleons, male or female; they climb over males in their path without incident. But a male presuming to short-cut over a female will receive a harsh bite as his reward. The female warns before attacking by rocking. She lifts one front leg, the opposite rear leg, and sways on the remaining two. A female defending her territory becomes pale as well. A defeated female, like a defeated male, becomes drab and runs away, dropping to the ground if pursued. Chameleons of other species are ignored and can pass unmolested.

Mating

Males initiate courtship rituals by head jerking. The head jerks sharply upward and returns to the original position more softly, at the rate of two jerks per second. The male may begin head jerking in the presence of several females without selecting one for particular attention, but eventually he focuses on a single female. The females sway in response, but a nearby male may react by attacking. After making his choice, the amorous reptile struts unevenly toward his chosen mate, head jerking all the while. The head movements continue until he successfully

On preceding page:
A male chameleon, like this aggressive C. calyptratus, *may rear up on his hind legs in combat with another male, or when reaching for a branch, as in this photograph.*

mounts her. Often, the female rejects the male's advances with hissing, posturing and bites. A rebuffed male loses his strut and ceases his head jerks for a while, but soon his confidence returns and he tries again. Sometimes he may make several approaches before the female acquiesces.

Like other mountain chameleons, *hoehnelii* are born live but are not truly viviparous. Baby chameleons develop in an egg inside the mother, who then delivers. The babies emerge encased in a thin sticky membrane, the remnants of the egg. Thus *hoehnelii* are ovoviviparous.

As the young pass down the birth canal, the mother swells for a moment. In 15 to 60 seconds she expels the baby, rubbing her cloaca against the branch so the diaphanous membrane adheres. After giving birth, she moves to another location, where she deposits another baby, thus dispersing the young. Two to six minutes later, she gives birth once more.

Although casque-headed chameleons aren't truly viviparous, their young enjoy the benefits of live birth. The eggs stay warm as their mother exercises her thermoregulatory powers, which is critical on the chilly mountain slopes. Because the mother lays each egg in a different place, animals intent on dining on young *hoehnelii* are unlikely to catch them all before they scatter. One brood may consist of 10 or so young, each about two inches long at birth.

Born in a tightly curled position with the tail stretched under the belly and across the face, the baby straightens and struggles to free itself. In less than 10 minutes, the animal escapes from the membrane, and within a few minutes its color changes from dirty beige without pattern to black marked with brown diamonds or stripes. Now suitably adorned, the baby marches off to begin a solitary life. The young are especially active the first few hours after birth. This activity further scatters the brood and guards against a single predator wiping out the siblings if detected in one place.

Except for color and heft, young *hoehnelii* resemble their parents. They adopt a dingy gray brown, resembling knots on the tree branches. When they are angry, faint patterns appear, but only with adulthood will the chameleons command a complete palette. Otherwise, they come equipped with all the skills necessary to survival: the erratic walk, the lightning tongue, the two 180-degree eyes.

Mouth gaping is common among contending males.
Here, C. oustaleti *makes threatening gestures.*

Nonetheless, the young face a world of terrors. Even adult *hoehnelii* are a threat. They sometimes capture the babies and administer a few tentative chews before rejecting them as food, but the young often sustain fatal injuries during these taste tests. Snakes, birds and insects feed on them, too.

Miraculously, a few survive to adulthood to perpetuate the species. Unlike some other species, the casque-headed chameleons have seemed able to adapt to the destruction of their forests, so far, moving onto crops and shrubbery. However, ravages to the environment may inadvertently trigger the decline and disappearance of the species at any time. Every species of chameleon is at risk from both predictable and hidden causes. Only good husbandry and stewardship on the planet will guarantee future generations the opportunity to find these tiny dragons hidden among the branches of Africa's high forests.

IN SEARCH OF SLOWFOOT: *CHAMAELEO PUMILUS*

At the southern tip of Africa lives the most troublesome chameleon, at least for taxonomists concerned with chameleon systematics. Depending on which authority is consulted, *Chamaeleo pumilus*, the African dwarf chameleon, and its closest relatives are a primitive example of the genus *Chamaeleo*—perhaps the mother of the genus—or a unique genus known by any number of names, or an intermediate animal poised between arboreal and terrestrial chameleons.

The *pumilus* chameleons are among the most colorful of the Chamaeleonidae family, bedecked in bright reds, rich turquoises and iridescent highlights. Fully arboreal, these tiny lizards parade through almost every niche in South Africa. They live in the rainy southeast, on the Drakensberg Plateau and on desert scrub.

Dutch taxonomist Dirk Hillenius considered all the dwarf chameleons of South Africa to be subspecies of *Chamaeleo pumilus*, including *Chamaeleo caffer, damaranus, gutturalis, karrooicus, melanocephalus, occidentalis, täeniobronchus, transvaalensis* and *ventralis*. He dubbed them the *pumilus* group. As always, variations in characteristics frustrated the taxonomist's quest for neat classification. For example, *Cham-*

aeleo pumilus transvaalensis has more in common with *ventralis* and *damaranus* than with the putative primary species, which shouldn't be the case if it were a subspecies of *pumilus.*

Before Hillenius, attempts to establish the dwarf's place in Chamaeleonidae suffered from more serious problems. The first man to describe them, the German naturalist Samuel Gmelin in 1789, placed *pumilus* among the *Lacerta,* a group of thin, colorful and fast lizards. Thirteen years later a French explorer, Daudin, correctly recognized them as chameleons. In 1864 Gray also characterized them as chameleons but perversely changed their name to *Lophosaura pumilus* while creating the genus *Microsaura* for their close cousins, *melanocephalus.* Since he had already named a group of South American lizards *Lophosaura,* this classification was confusing to say the least, yet it wasn't universally discarded until 1943.

Thereafter, one camp of scientists included *pumilus* among *Microsaura* while others insisted the group belonged in the family Chamaeleonidae. Most *Microsaura* champions worked in South Africa, and one detects a provincial pride in their defense of their unique group of chameleons.

Adherents of the *Chamaeleo* party trundled out their arguments. The *pumilus* hemipenes is the cogwheel type, similar to the flapneck chameleon (*C. dilepis*), the *Chamaeleo* species with the widest range in Africa, including the habitat of the *pumilus.* The *pumilus* shoulder girdle resembles *Chamaeleo* more than the other two chameleon genera, *Brookesia* or *Rhampholeon.*

Dissenters noted that several distinct characteristics bind the group together and argue for a separate genus. The dwarves possess smooth, simple lungs; the hemipenes are relatively simple. Although bone structure is closer to *Chamaeleo* than the terrestrial dwarves, it still differs substantially.

Modern proponents of the separate genus call the group *Bradypodion,* or "slowfoot." Hillenius's scientific rival, Klaver, accepts the establishment of a new genus and includes similar northern species within the genus, including *xenorhinus* and *carpenteri* from the Mountains of the Moon.

Predators and Competitors

Pumilus chameleons provide food for a host of animals. Several genera of snakes venture into the branches for a snack. Birds of prey pluck them from their perches. Shrikes drape the corpses on barbed wire fences to eat at their convenience. Near human settlements dogs and especially cats feed upon them. Young *pumilus* sometimes fall victim to the larger flap-necked chameleons and spiders eat the very young.

In addition to the threat of predators, *pumilus* suffer from intestinal parasites, especially nematodes. In the summer almost every individual carries the parasite, but less than one-fifth have them in the cooler months.

The dwarves are often unable to compete with other species that choose to occupy their habitat. Ground-dwelling skinks sometimes climb the larger plants inhabited by the chameleons, driving the tiny lizards away and eating the young chameleons. Geckos live on mountain conifers that the chameleons could use, thus consigning the *pumilus* to shrubs.

Thermoregulation

Winters in South Africa resemble conditions found on Mount Kenya, home of the casque-headed chameleon, *C. hoehnelii*. Although South Africa receives much less rain, temperatures can drop to near freezing. Even when the mercury falls to near freezing, the *pumilus* remain active, still able to catch insects on the fly. Heavy rain that drives other reptiles "indoors" doesn't deter the chameleons. They are partially endothermic; that is, they are somewhat warm-blooded. However, researchers have found that temperatures of 20° F sustained for two hours will kill them.

The *pumilus* employs the same techniques as its cousins to absorb heat: lateral flattening, darkening, inflation of air sacs, sequential blood warming (see p. 56). It can turn darker than most chameleons, thus absorbing more sunlight quickly, which is critical in its cooler environment. The animal uses these tactics in the early morning, near sunset and whenever warmth is available on chilly days. It tends to sun in the lee of the wind and will press against a warm object, such as a rock that has absorbed heat, to increase its temperature. These techniques allow the animal to raise its body temperature above the environmental temperature.

At the warm end of its thermal tolerance, the *pumilus* again uses common reptilian techniques, such as panting, to dissipate heat. Extra blood flows to the tongue for additional evaporative cooling, and the side of the body facing the sun turns to a lighter color to reflect heat.

Adjusting temperature puts the chameleon at risk. As it absorbs heat in its flattened position and unpatterned coloration, it could appear more conspicuous to predators. Several factors, however, reduce the danger. The dark side of the body faces the sky, so birds of prey see only the non-reflective side of the reptile on a dark green background, while predators on the ground face the lighter side blending with the sky. Finally, the chameleon's crests and knobs break up the animal's outline, making it harder to see. A *pumilus* trying to dissipate heat loses every advantage except its irregular outline.

While the dwarves can tolerate temperature extremes, they enjoy warm temperatures. At about 75° F the lizards can stop regulating their own temperature and concentrate on other activities. At these temperatures the animal assumes its most effective camouflaging colors and patterns.

Reproduction

With the dwarves, love is always in the air. Courtship and mating occur above ground, and mating occurs 10 months of the year. The male holds one branch firmly with his tail as he conducts his mating dance, a specific set of horizontal head bobs and weaves. He wears his brightest green while the female dresses down, maintaining a modest dark shade. If the female tolerates him, mating commences and will last about 10 minutes. Sexual relations may be repeated several times a day, several days per week. When the mating concludes, the female's mood shifts from passive to hostile. She will remain aggressive until bearing her young.

The *pumilus* group has adopted the same reproductive strategy, ovoviviparous live birth, as the *bitaeniatus* group, the only other group to do so. Given the relatively cool conditions in which these groups live, the eggs have a better chance of coming to term in the mother's body. She may deliver four clutches each year.

The female gives birth to between five and 10 young. They may be born one second apart or as much as eight minutes apart. Each youngster frees itself within a minute and some escape from the yolk sac before birth. They all begin their independent careers immediately.

A Day in the Life

Dwarf chameleons stir before sunrise, moving slowly after a night in the open. The pale coloration of night darkens and they begin to hunt. When the sun's rays first hit them, they perform their thermoregulatory tricks and then venture, fully charged, into the world. During light rain or showers the schedule remains the same, but major storms drive them into thick underbrush, probably to minimize heat loss from wind chill.

Pumilus spend most of the day hunting. Instead of actively patrolling for food, they position themselves on plants and fences to ambush unwary prey. They can be found on all sorts of vegetation likely to attract insects, from bushes to evergreens, but favor reeds bordering standing or stagnant water. So far as anyone knows, these lizards can't swim; the lizards have traded a safe perch for access to plentiful food.

The tongue can capture prey at a distance two-thirds of the chameleon's total length, and the tongue can pull prey half of the chameleon's weight. The lizards aren't fussy eaters, but they like variety. They feed on different insects as the seasons change, and they always eat to capacity if possible. They drink by lapping water droplets from leaves or from their own bodies. *Pumilus* have been seen to zap drops with their tongue, too. In summer they depend on dew. They always drink early in the day.

Like the Namaqua, the *pumilus* feed on dangerous prey and learn ways to avoid harm. They use different techniques for each prey, such as chewing off stingers from scorpions or seizing vipers behind the head to elude the fangs. The young puzzle out safe hunting techniques by trial and error in just a few days, if they survive their errors.

When confronted by a threat, the *pumilus* chameleons react atypically. Instead of remaining still, in an effort to appear invisible, they try to hide behind twigs and branches. Their movement is likely to attract attention, however. If their first tactic fails, they drop to the ground or walk briskly, for a chameleon, away from the threat. When confronted by another lizard of a different species, they may perform territorial displays to warn the intruder away. If caught by a human, they bite without effect.

The sight of another chameleon provokes a more typically aggressive reaction, especially among females. The aggrieved lizard expands its throat to expose veins of either purple or orange interstitial skin. Lateral compression and turning the side of the body 90 degrees to the intruder enhances the illusion of unusual size. Five head bobs describing a "T," executed with great precision in less than one-and-a-half seconds, represents the final warning before an attack. If the intruder fails to yield, the chameleon will charge and bite. Sometimes both chameleons lose their grip and fall to earth. Injuries are common but death is rare.

Pumilus only defend the area where they sleep. Otherwise, they tend to wander over large areas in the treetops without much conflict, although most movement is vertical. Young *pumilus* have no territory whatever to defend, and they roam over very large areas both horizontally and vertically.

As night falls the heart slows and the body pales once more. Both actions retard heat loss. The chameleon finds an exposed perch where the sun will likely strike first and goes to sleep.

CHAMELEONS
IN
CAPTIVITY

Given the strange charm and beauty of chameleons, it's no wonder they are in demand in the pet trade. With their goofy gait, pop-eyed stares, magical color changes and startling tongue, they are stars of the terrarium. Only one thing detracts from their appeal in captivity: They die.

Watching any pet die hurts, but chameleons have special tortures for those who care for them. Usually they refuse food and eventually water. Week by week they waste away, eyes sinking in their skulls and a gray pallor dulling their skin. Just before death brilliant, hitherto unseen colors tint the body. Soon the chameleon lies inert on the bottom of its enclosure.

Once the decline starts even experts have trouble reversing the trend. Usually the deterioration started before the animal arrived in its owner's care. In the wild chameleons play host to parasites. In its own habitat with familiar food the lizards feel few ill effects from the freeloaders, but the stress of capture, transport and incarceration weakens them.

Considering the ill-treatment they receive at the hands of hunters, distributors, shippers and pet store employees, it's amazing any survive. Natives who fear them yet are anxious for a day's pay rip them from their branches and toss them in a sack. Chameleons grip so tightly their bones break before they release the branch. Often several of the highly unsocial reptiles share a sack where they can't escape contact. They pose, display and fight with no exit available. After days in cramped conditions with little or no food or water, jostled by awful Third World roads, baked by sun and bitten by fellow captives, they arrive at the distributors, where they may languish for weeks in squalid conditions. Eventually they will be picked for a flight to an animal distributor in Europe or the United States. Many die before being loaded on the plane, but many more succumb in freezing holds, unventilated boxes or broiling on the tropical tarmac. Not every baggage handler treats them with the tenderness they deserve. When the stateside distributor receives his weakened cargo, it's already too late for many. No amount of rehydration, medication or food will compensate for the stress.

In due course some make it to pet stores. Many employees, untutored in the art of chameleon care, often do everything wrong, from feeding them vegetables to providing water in a dish when most species only lick moisture from leaves. Often you find them still crowded together inside a terrarium in a state of unrelenting and exhausting display. There are happy exceptions to this story, but most of the time chameleons found in pet stores need a rehabilitation program beyond the means of typical pet owners.

To increase the odds of survival, reputable importers gather the reptiles themselves or with trained assistance. The animals receive ample food and water. Medication purges them of parasites before shipping and the importer flies with his cargo. Upon arrival, an aggressive program of rehydration, supplementation and medication begins. The odds on finding such a pampered chameleon in a pet store, however, is next to nil; therefore a simple rule applies: Wild-caught chameleons should never be kept as pets.

The rationale against keeping wild chameleons as pets is compelling. First, your pet will almost certainly die within a few months at best. Second, it encourages exportation, which kills thousands of chameleons to no purpose and increases the chances of extinction for already hard-pressed species.

The only defensible reason for importing chameleons is to create or participate in captive breeding programs. With ever-shrinking habitats, many species may survive only through the efforts of herpetoculturists. As the forests of Madagascar fall and the African brush burns to make room for crops, the future of many varieties may reside in the backyards of lizard fanciers and in zoos dedicated to chameleon propagation.

So far only a few species have prospered in captivity. Several generations of *pardalis* have prospered and some are entering the pet trade. The gaudy Yemenese *calyptratus* and the giant Meller's wait in the wings. Jackson's have been bred and some appear on the market from Hawaii, descendants of terrarium escapees. But some of the most attractive species, such as the giant Parson's, have not succeeded in captivity. The conditions needed to hatch their eggs remain unknown, and the conditions most oviparous species need are a mystery.

It is now possible, however, to obtain captive-born chameleons, and their beauty makes them hard to resist. Each species lives by a different set of rules, and often the rules are unpublished. However, some general rules apply.

- Chameleons prefer very large enclosures. If the temperature of the room is appropriate, giving them the run of

Though tempting as pets, chameleons do poorly in captivity. Despite its large size, the beautiful Parson's chameleon pictured here is highly vulnerable.

the house may be best. They tend to pick one plant or fixture as their territory, but you need to be alert when they wander. People with free-roaming chameleons have found them in dishwashers, washing machines and squeezed behind furniture. Keeping them in a wire cage outdoors is even better. In the southern United States, Jackson's, which like temperature swings, thrive outside. Natural sunlight helps, too. The efficacy of grow-lites as a sun substitute for reptiles is unproven. Only frosts drive them inside. Watch a chameleon battling the glass of a small enclosure to get out. Even if you try to suppress anthropomorphic feelings, they still seem frustrated and confused.

• Most chameleons need temperature changes. Even a 10- or 15-degree variation will do the trick for most. Temperature requirements differ by species. A Parson's shouldn't dip below 65° F while Jackson's flourish down to 40° F.

- Spray them with water. A few individuals will drink from a dish but many will literally die first. They lick moisture off glass or leaves or just let it drip off their heads and into their mouths. Some learn to drink from the spray bottle itself, which helps the keeper regulate the amount of water they receive. Water them twice a day if possible, except for desert species. Lack of water probably directly kills more captive chameleons than any other cause.
- Keep males separated. Even if they don't harass one another, the constant low-level stress will leave them susceptible to disease.
- Chameleons need a varied diet. Fortified meal worms, beetles, cockroaches, crickets and flies keep them interested. They will eventually refuse food if it's the same day after day. Dust the food with reptile vitamins. Some shy chameleons won't eat if you watch, while others pluck insects from your hand. Feed them only live food.

Clearly, chameleons demand much more attention and care than a typical pet. They require space, a diverse diet, temperature variations, parasite removal and peculiar watering. Because many species are threatened, only captive-bred animals should be considered as pets, to eliminate hunting pressure on wild populations. The first law of chameleon husbandry should echo the physician's motto, "First, do no harm."

APPENDIXES

APPENDIX I
THE CHAMAELEONIDAE
FAMILY—TAXONOMIES

There are more than 100 species in the Chamaeleonidae family, which is then subdivided into several genera. Rival taxonomies assign chameleons to many different genera. For example, one system considers all ground-dwelling chameleons with limited prehensile tails to be part of the genus *Brookesia*, while another system divides the group into four genera. The genus *Chamaeleo* suffers from similar confusion.

Dirk Hillenius herded *Chamaeleo* into groups with similar characteristics, e.g., *pumilus:* South African ovoviviparous dwarf chameleons; *cucullatus:* Madagascar species with large occipital lobes. Klaver also created groupings, often very different from Hillenius's, but he defined each group as a separate genus or subgenus with perhaps too little foundation. When the text refers to a group, it refers to the Hillenius taxonomic groups. The two systems can be broken down as follows:

FAMILY CHAMAELEONIDAE

Genus Chamaeleo

Madagascar Species

Rhinoceratus group: labordi, monoceras, barbouri, voeltzlowi, rhinoceratus, and lineatus. Rare Madagascar chameleons distinguished by a rigid, laterally compressed rostral appendage. Defined by Hillenius based on 13 specimens. They could be closely related to *xenorhinus.*

Lateralis group: lateralis, campani, lambertoni. Distinguished from other Madagascar chameleons by the double row of scales on the dorsal keel, the absence of occipital lobes and the presence of a white line down the side.

Oustaleti group: oustaleti, verrucosus, semicristatus, pardalis, guentheri. Madagascar species distinguished by coarse, heterogeneous squamation, prominent parietal crest, highly elevated casque, no occipital lobes and large size.

Nasutus group: nasutus, fallax, gallus, boettgeri, linotus, guibei. Madagascar species distinguished by flexible rostral appendix (absent only in the females of linotus), absence of any but the rostral crest and small size, the smallest of the genus *Chamaeleo*. Because of their resemblance to the dwarf chameleons *Brookesia* and *Rhampholeon,* specifically their small size and flexible rostral appendices, they may be transitional species.

Cucullatus group: cucullatus, malthe, brevicornis. Madagascar species distinguished by large occipital lobes. Males possess small, paired rostral protuberances.

Parsonii group: parsonii, globifer, oshaughnessyi. Madagascar chameleons distinguished by a broad, flat casque and a lack of crests. Males possess laterally compressed rostral protuberances.

Bifidus group: bifidus, minor, willsi. Madagascar chameleons distinguished by a flat casque, absence of occipital lobes and single or paired white lines under the tail and along the midventral line. Males have two rigid, short, laterally compressed rostral protuberances.

African, European and Asian Species

Chamaeleon group: chamaeleon, calcarifer, zeylanicus, calyptratus, basilicus, laevigatus, senegalensis, gracilis, etiennei, dilepis, angusticoronatus. Distinguished by an absence of crests, keels, horns, etc. All possess even scales and a white midventral line; most have dorsal crests.

Oweni group: oweni, unicornis, michelli. African chameleons distinguished by a double row of scales on the dorsal keel, homogeneous squamation, a tail much longer than the head and body together and one to three cranial horns.

Johnstoni group: johnstoni, ituriensis. Distinguished by heterogeneous squamation, tail the same length as the body and the absence of occipital lobes.

Bitaeniatus group: bitaeniatus, jacksoni, tempeli, werneri, fuelleborni. Distinguished by a parietal crest forked in the front, a dorsal crest of unequal cones, the absence of a gular crest or a crest formed by ordinary cones. Jacksoni and bitaeniatus lack occipital lobes. Members are ovoviviparous, small to moderate size and possess roughly heterogeneous squamation.

Pumilus group: pumilus, melanocephalus, gutteralis, taeniobronchus, ventralis, damaranus, caffer. These small- to medium-sized ovoviviparous lizards share coarse, heterogeneous squamation and usually lack ventral crests. They are found only in South Africa.

***Genus* Brookesia** (Hillenius doesn't define *Brookesia* systematics.)

Unlike Hillenius, Klaver and Böhme didn't depend on similar external characteristics to group chameleons. Instead, they looked to similarities in hemipenis and lung morphologies.

Because the characteristics they use are impossible to see on a living specimen, I've elected to list their system without cataloging the technical details defining each group. Consult their papers listed in the bibliography for a full exposition of their system.

KLAVER AND BÖHME SYSTEM

FAMILY CHAMAELEONIDAE

SUBFAMILY BROOKESIINAE

Genus **Brookesia**

Species: antoetrae, betschi, bonsi, decaryi, dentata, ebenaui, griveaudi, karchei, lambertoni, legendrei, minima, nasus, peyrierasi, ramanantsoai, stumpffi, supercilliaris, therezieni, theili, tuberculata, vadoni

Genus **Rhampholeon**

Species: brachyurus, brevicaudatus, kerstenii, marshalli, nchisiensis, platyceps, spectrum, temporalis

SUBFAMILY CHAMAELEONIDAE

Madagascar

Genus **Calumma**

Species: boettgeri, brevicornis, capuroni, cucullata, fallax, furcifer, gallus, gastrotaenia, globifer, fuibei, linota, malthe, nasutus, oshaughnessyi, parsonii, peyrierasi, tsaratananensis, tigris

Genus **Furcifer**

Species: angeli, antimena, balteatus, belalandaensis, bifidus, campani, cephalolepis, labordi, lateralis, minor, monoceras, oustaleti, pardalis, petteri, polleni, rhinoceratus, tuzetae, verrucosus, willsi

Africa

Genus Bradypodion

Species: adolfifrederici, caffer, carpenteri, damatanum, dracomontanum, fischeri, gutterale, karroicum, melanocephalum, mlanjense, nemorale, occidentale, pumilum, setaroi, spinosum, taeniobronchum, tenue, thamnobates, uthmoelleri, ventrale, xenorhinum

Genus Chamaeleo

Subgenus Chamaeleo

Species: africanus, arabicus, anchietae, calcaricaren, calyptratus, chamaeleon, dilepis, gracilis, laevigatus, monachus, namaquensis, quilensis, senegalensis, zeylanicus

Subgenus Triceros

Species: affinis, bitaeniatus, camerunensis, chapini, cristatus, deremensis, eisentrauti, ellioti, feae, fuelleborni, goetzi, hoehnelii, incornutus, jacksonii, johnstoni, kinetensis, laterispinis, melleri, montium, oweni, pfefferi, quadricornus, rudis, schoutendeni, schubotzi, tempeli, werneri, wiedersheimi

APPENDIX II
A SPECIES-BY-SPECIES LIST
OF THE WORLD'S
CHAMELEONS

The following list recognizes only three genera. I've elected to distinguish only two ground dwellers, the *Brookesia* (stump-tailed chameleons) of Madagascar and the *Rhampholeon* (leaf chameleons) of Africa. I've ignored the debate regarding the subdivision of *Chamaeleo* except to note those species that resemble the dwarf chameleons of South Africa and their few far flung cousins to the north, the so-called *Bradypodion* genus. These chameleons have unusually simple lungs and hemipenes and slightly different bone structure, but they possess *Chamaeleo*'s characteristic prehensile tail and survival strategies, so they remain lumped with their larger arboreal brethren in the following list.

The information on particular chameleons varies considerably, and papers concerning them are rare in the United States. Where possible, the species name is followed by a general description of the animal, the naturalist who first described it, the date of its first appearance in the scientific literature and its known range.

Finally, a note on abbreviations. A capital letter followed by a period indicates the genus, e.g., *C.=Chamaeleo*, *B.=Brookesia*, and *R.=Rhampholeon*. A lowercase "c" means "chameleon."

GENUS CHAMAELEO

Chamaeleo adolfifrederici

Description: Dorsal crest runs halfway down the back or is absent. Short snout in males and weakly elevated casque. Isolated conical tubercles on the faint parietal and lateral crests. A small chameleon first found in the Ituri Forest of the Pygmies. Usually forest green with black spots, turns dark when angry and light green when triumphant in battle. Similar to *Bradypodion* tenue. Placed among *Bradypodion* by Klaver and Böhme, 1986. First described by Sternfeld, 1912.

Distribution: Zaire, Rwanda, Uganda

Chamaeleo affinis

Description: A desert chameleon with homogeneous squamation, flat casque, no gular crest, lateral row of larger shields on the flank and an indistinct groove on the upper lip from nostril to nostril. It was considered the same as *C. J. Johnstoni* by Mertens, 1966, but resurrected by Klaver and Böhme, 1986. First described by Ruppell, 1845.

Distribution: Ethiopia and Somalia

Chamaeleo africanus
AFRICAN CHAMELEON

Description: Drab coloration. Very similar to *C. chamaeleon chamaeleon* but with a more elevated casque. Becomes dormant in December and January. Grows to 14 inches. First described by Laurenti, 1768.

Distribution: Somalia to Egypt (including the Nile delta) and west to Cameroon and Nigeria

C. bitaeniatus, *the two-lined chameleon.*

Chamaeleo anchietae anchietae

Description: Very similar to *C. laevigatus.* Possesses a double row of scales on the dorsal keel and a gular crest. Grows to 6 inches. First described by Bocage, 1872.

Distribution: Angola

Chamaeleo angeli

Description: Brick-colored, with a white stripe on the sides. Minimal gular crest and pronounced dorsal crest. Single rigid rostral protuberance (similar to *C. brevicornis*), distinct parietal crest and a low casque. Heterogeneous squamation. Lives in rain forest. Males grow to 13 inches. First described by Brygoo and Domergue, 1968.

Distribution: Northwest Madagascar, north of Tsaramandroso, Ankarafantsika forest

Chamaeleo angusticoronatus

Description: Similar to *dilepis.* First described by Barbour, 1903. Placed in *C. dilepis* by Mertens, 1966.

Distribution: Zanzibar

Chamaeleo antimena

Description: Once considered the same as *C. rhinoceratus*, this green chameleon is distinguished by a white line in the middle of the ventral surface and a concave rostral appendix. A low, sharply defined casque with parietal, orbital and lateral crests; heterogeneous squamation. Large, curved, irregular cones on the dorsal crest. Grows to 7 inches. First described by Grandidier, 1872; resurrected by Brygoo and Domergue, 1968.

Distribution: Southwest Madagascar

Chamaeleo balteatus

Description: A forest dweller once considered the same as *C. bifidus*. Homogeneous squamation, two rostral appendices on the males. Distinct lateral and orbital crest, but no parietal crest. No occipital lobes or gular crest; small, short dorsal crest. Predominantly drab green, sometimes with white marks and blackish transverse stripes. Grows to 15 inches. First described by Dumeril and Bibron, 1851; studied closely by Brygoo and Domergue, 1969.

Distribution: Madagascar, between Ifanadiana and Fort Carnot in the eastern rain forest.

Chamaeleo barbouri

Description: A member of the *C. rhinoceratus* group, it has a single rigid, laterally compressed rostral protuberance, white coloration under the tail and a parietal crest. First described by Hechenbleikner, 1942. Considered the same as *C. labordi* by Brygoo and Domergue, 1968.

Distribution: Madagascar

Chamaeleo belalandaensis

Description: Green with a dirty white lateral line. Grows to five inches. Tiny rostral appendage. Small gular and large dorsal crest, distinct parietal and ocular crests. First described by Brygoo and Domergue, 1970.

Distribution: Southwest Madagascar; Belalanda, just north of Tulear

Chamaeleo bifidus

Description: A rain forest species distinguished by a flat casque, absence of occipital lobes and single white line under the tail. Predominantly green. Males have two rigid, short, laterally compressed, parallel rostral protuberances. Often has a low, lateral white band. Grows to 15 inches. First described by Brongniart, 1800.

Distribution: Eastern and north-central Madagascar

Chamaeleo bitaeniatus bitaeniatus
TWO-LINED CHAMELEON

Description: Two stripes run down the sides, which also feature sporadic spots. Ovoviviparous. Roughly heterogeneous squamation, moderate to small size, parietal crest forked in front, ventral and gular crest present, dorsal crest with unequal cones. No occipital lobes. Grows to 6 inches. First described by Fischer, 1884.

Distribution: Ethiopia, Kenya, Somalia, Uganda, northern and western Tanzania and eastern Zaire

Chamaeleo bitaeniatus ellioti

Description: Ovoviviparous. Roughly heterogeneous squamation, moderate to small size, parietal crest forked in front, gular and ventral crest present, dorsal crest with equal cones. First described by Günther, 1895.

Distribution: Sudan, Kenya, Tanzania, Rwanda, Uganda, Burundi and eastern Zaire

Chamaeleo boettgeri
BOETTGER'S CHAMELEON

Description: Similar to *C. nasutus*. Fused occipital lobes and a smoother head than *nasutus*. Low casque with dermal fold posteriorly. Upper scales vary in size; smooth scales elsewhere. Compressed, scaled, rounded, flexible rostral appendage. Pale green. Grows to 4 inches. First described by Boulenger, 1888.

Distribution: Northern Madagascar and Nosy Be

On the following page:
C. bifidus *has a flat casque and two lateral ridges.*

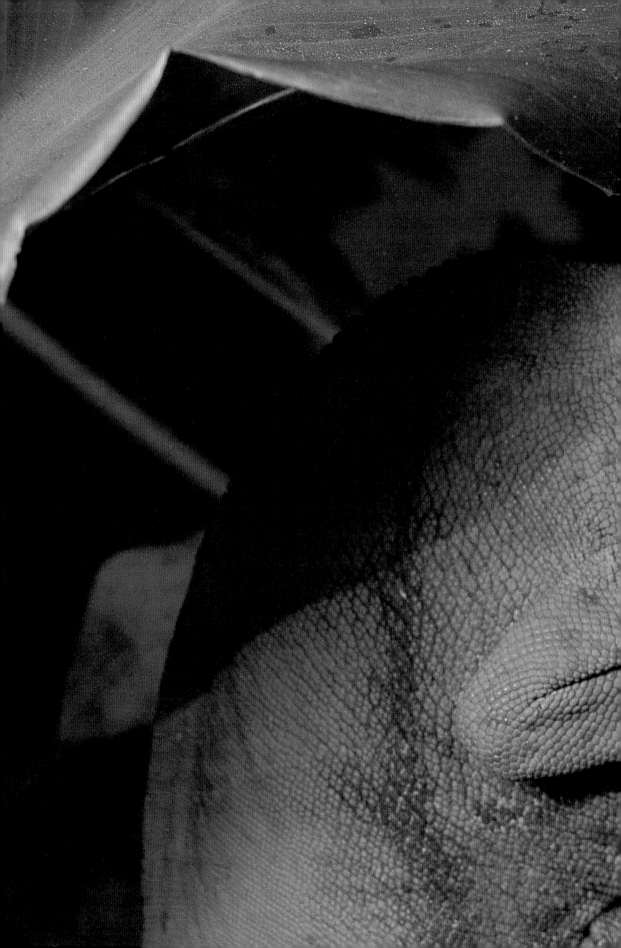

Chamaeleo brevicornis brevicornis
SHORT-HORNED CHAMELEON

Description: A member of the *cucullatus* group. Both a short horn, which males use as a battering ram in territorial fights, and articulating flaps, which they can move independently. Usually brown, but ranges from white to almost black. Tubercular lateral crest, distinct parietal crest, distinct dorsal crest. Sometimes transverse rows of cones on the throat and belly. Lives near the ground. Nine inches to 13 inches. First described by Günther, 1879.

Distribution: Near Perinet, eastern Madagascar. Also central, south-central and Montagne D'Ambre

Chamaeleo brevicornis hilleniusi

Description: Both a short horn and articulating flaps. First described by Brygoo, Blanc and Domergue, 1973.

Distribution: Madagascar

Chamaeleo brevicornis tsarafidyi

Description: A short rostral process and smaller occipital lobes. No parietal crest. First described by Brygoo and Domergue, 1970.

Distribution: Ankafana, Madagascar

Chamaeleo calyptratus

Description: An aggressive, brightly colored chameleon with a very high, laterally compressed casque, almost 2 inches high. Four to five vertical bands split before reaching the dorsal keel. Very long cones on the gular crest. Closely related to *C. chamaeleon* (Hillenius, 1966). Lives on Yemen's high, dry plateau. Grows to 15 inches. First described by Dumeril, 1851.

Distribution: Near Sana, Yemen

Chamaeleo calyptratus calcarifer

Description: Similar to *C. calyptratus* with smaller casque. Once thought a hybrid of *C. calyptratus* and *C. c. arabicus* by Hillenius (1966), now regarded as distinct (Hillenius, 1986). First described by Peters, 1854.

Distribution: Near the border of Yemen and Saudi Arabia along the foot of the escarpment, to an elevation of nearly 3,000 feet

Chamaeleo campani

Description: Similar to *C. lateralis.* Mid-ventral white stripe, double row of scales on the dorsal keel, no occipital lobes. Two or more white lines on the sides. Prefers high forest. Grows to about 5 inches. First described by Grandidier, 1872.

Distribution: Central Madagascar

Chamaeleo capuroni

Description: First described by Brygoo, Blanc and Domergue, 1972.

Distribution: Madagascar

Chamaeleo carpenteri

Description: Giant casque with pronounced, curved parietal crest incut at the base. Canthal crests becomes pointed, bifurcated rostral appendices on the males. Heterogeneous squamation. Grows to 11 inches. First described by Parker, 1929.

Distribution: Ruwenzori Mountains, Zaire and Uganda

Chamaeleo cephalolepis

Description: Lacks protuberances, conspicuous crests or occipital lobes. Homogeneous squamation. Unlike the closely related *C. polleni,* possesses gular crest. First described by Günther, 1880.

Distribution: Mayotte and Grand Comoro, Comoro Islands

Chamaeleo chamaeleon arabicus

Description: Homogeneous squamation. High casque with crest of scales in back. Prefers elevations below 1,800 feet. First described by Matschie, 1893.

Distribution: Lahej, near Aden, Yemen

On following page:
The tiny C. boettgeri *is similar to* C. nasutus.

Chamaeleo chamaeleon chamaeleon
EUROPEAN or COMMON CHAMELEON

Description: Homogeneous squamation. Tarsal spurs present. Lives in burrows it digs. Yellow-brown coloration. Grows to 11 inches long. First described by the biologist Linnaeus in 1758, although Aristotle's chameleon may have been the same species.

Distribution: North coast of Africa, islands of the Mediterranean (including Cyprus and Crete), the southern tip of Spain, Turkey and the western Middle East

Chamaeleo chamaeleon musae

Description: Closely related to *C. c. orientalis*, differentiated by a straight parietal crest, the greatest width of the occipital flap occurs on the lower third, and the flap has fewer scales than *orientalis* (five to six, instead of seven to eight). First described by Steindachner, 1900.

Distribution: Western Saudi Arabia

Chamaeleo chamaeleon orientalis

Description: A desert chameleon with six to seven dark vertical bands on the dorsal half of the body split before reaching the dorsal keel. Curved parietal crest. First described by Parker, 1938.

Distribution: Western Arabia from Haql on the Gulf of Aqaba south, at the highest elevations into Yemen, to almost the 14th parallel. Prefers elevations above 6,000 feet although sometimes found as low as 3,000 feet. *C. calyptratus* and *C. chamaeleon arabicus* occupy the lower elevations to the south and southwest.

Chamaeleo chamaeleon recticrista

Description: A desert chameleon with homogeneous squamation and an absence of conspicuous characters. First described by Boettger, 1880.

Distribution: Sinai Peninsula

Chamaeleo chamaeleon zeylanicus

Description: High casque with arching parietal bone. Ventral crest and dorsal crest from neck to tail. All males and some females possess tarsal spurs. An 8-inch lizard. First described by Laurenti, 1768.

Distribution: Southern India and Sri Lanka. Isolated from the territories of other chameleons by over 600 miles.

Chamaeleo chapini

Description: Homogeneous squamation. Faintly elevated casque. Gray with blackish oblique marks. No dorsal, gular, parietal or ventral crests. Grows to 6 inches. First described by Witte, 1964.

Distribution: Zaire

Chamaeleo cristatus
CRESTED CHAMELEON

Description: Eight to 9 inches. Possesses a high serrated dorsal crest. Usually emerald green with yellow-red gular pouch. First described by Stutchburg, 1837.

Distribution: Nigeria, Gabon, Equatorial Guinea, lowland areas near Mt. Cameroon

Chamaeleo cucullatus

Description: This rare rain forest species possesses a spine-like extension connected on both sides of the large, fused occipital lobes. Males are light gray with a large, reddish-yellow mark longitudinally; females are a uniform green. Dubbed the "hooded chameleon" by its discoverer. Grows to 15 inches. First described by Gray, 1831.

Distribution: Eastern Madagascar

Chamaeleo damaranus
KNYSNA DWARF CHAMELEON

Description: Larger scales in lateral rows on flank. High casque. Scaled, compressed, overlapping gular crest. Prominent cranial crests. Males are bright emerald green with blue to maroon patches on the flanks and yellow around the forelimbs. Cranial crests are yellow to blue. Lives in wet coastal forests. Ovoviviparous. Also known

On following page:
C. campani, *a Madagascar species.*

as *Bradypodion damaranum* or Knysna dwarf chameleon. Grows to 6 inches. First described by Boulenger, 1887.

Distribution: Knysna and Avontuur districts, Southern Cape Province, South Africa

Chamaeleo deremensis

Description: Wavy dorsal fin, fused occipital lobes. First described by Matschie, 1892.

Distribution: Usambara and Uluguru mountains, Tanzania

Chamaeleo dilepis dilepis
FLAP-NECKED or COMMON CHAMELEON

Description: Flap-necked chameleons grow from 9 to 14 inches. The sobriquet "Common" refers to their numbers south of the Sahara, not to their resemblance to the European variety. Closely aligned with *Chamaeleo chamaeleon.* Pronounced, mobile occipital lobes. Gular crest, ventral crest and lateral crest well-developed. Males have tarsal spurs and orange interstitial skin on the throat pouch. Grows to 14 inches. First described by Leach, 1819.

Distribution: Cameroon to coastal Kenya and south to Botswana, northern Namibia and northeastern South Africa

Chamaeleo dilepis idjwiensis

Description: Distinguished by the lack of tarsal spurs and more pronounced gular crest. First described by Loveridge, 1942.

Distribution: Rwanda, Burundi and far eastern Zaire

Chamaeleo dilepis isabellinus

Description: First recorded by Günther, 1895.

Distribution: Shire Highlands of Malawi

Chamaeleo dilepis petersii

Description: First described by Gray, 1864.

Distribution: Mozambique and southern Tanzania

Chamaeleo dilepis quilensis

Description: Sometimes considered a subspecies of *C. dilepis.* Small, fused occipital lobes. Gular crest and

One of the handsomest chameleons, C. calyptratus.

lateral crest evident. Grows to 11 inches. First described by Bocage, 1866.

Distribution: Togo east to Kenya, south to Zimbabwe (including the Vumba Mountains) and to Botswana and South Africa (Natal, Transvaal, Swaziland and Kwazulu)

Chamaeleo dilepis roperi

Description: Sometimes classified as a subspecies of *C. dilepis*. Distinct parietal crest. Small but distinct and mobile occipital lobes. Gular and dorsal crests present. No tarsal spurs. Grows to 10 inches. First described by Boulenger, 1890.

Distribution: Zaire, Tanzania, Kenya, Angola

Chamaeleo dilepis ruspolii

Description: First described by Boettger, 1893.

Distribution: Somalia

Chamaeleo dracomontanum
DRAKENSBERG DWARF CHAMELEON

Description: Small recurved casque. Lateral dorsal and gular crests present. Males are greenish blue with dark markings on the flanks. White tubercles dot the sides. Ventral area marked in yellow. Females are green, white and brown. Lives in evergreen forest and high grassland. Also known as *Bradypodion dracomontanum.* First described by Raw, 1976.

Distribution: Southern and central Drakensberg Mountains, South Africa

Chamaeleo eisentrauti

Description: A rain forest chameleon first described by Mertens, 1968.

Distribution: Dikume, Rumpi Mountains, Cameroon

Chamaeleo fallax

Description: A member of the *nasutus* group. Single, short (⅛ of an inch), flexible and scale-covered rostral appendix. Slightly elevated casque. Heterogeneous squamation. Males possess dorsal and parietal crests. Grows to 4 inches. First described by Moquard, 1900.

Distribution: The central plateau, east coast and southeastern quadrant of Madagascar

Chamaeleo fischeri excubitor

Description: First described by Barbour, 1911.

Distribution: Mt. Kenya

Chamaeleo fischeri fischeri
FISCHER'S CHAMELEON

Description: Ovoviviparous. Roughly heterogeneous squamation, moderate to small size, parietal crest forked in front, gular and ventral crest present, dorsal crest with unequal cones. A very aggressive chameleon, it grows a flat horn that it uses to stab rivals. It reaches 13 inches. First described by Reichenow, 1887.

Distribution: Eastern and western Usambara Mountains, south to Nguru Mountains of Tanzania

Chamaeleo fischeri multituberculatus

Description: From the name we can deduce that this *fischeri* has large round scales on its flanks. First described by Neiden, 1913.

Distribution: Western Usambara Mountains, Tanzania

Chamaeleo fischeri tavetanus

Description: First described by Steindachner, 1891.

Distribution: Teita Mountains, Kenya to Mt. Kilimanjaro

Chamaeleo fischeri uluguruensis

Description: First described by Loveridge, 1956.

Distribution: Uluguru Mountains, Tanzania

Chamaeleo fischeri uthmolleri

Description: First described by Muller, 1938.

Distribution: Mt. Hanang, central Tanzania

Chamaeleo fuelleborni

Description: A member of the *bitaeniatus* group. Ovovivipa- rous. Rough heterogeneous squamation, moderate to small size, parietal crest forked in front, gular crest and ventral crest present, dorsal crest with unequal cones. "V"-shaped gular squamation on large occipital lobes. Three horns as in *jacksonii* but the body is plumper. Lives in highland forest. First described by Tornier, 1900.

Distribution: Ngosi Volcano, Poroto Mountains, Tanzania

Chamaeleo furcifer
FORK-NOSED CHAMELEON

Description: Sports a single, forked rostral protuberance cov- ered with scales. A double white line extends along the throat and ventral surface of the body to the middle of the tail. No casque or crests and poorly developed occipital lobes. Grows to just 5 inches. First described by Vaillant and Grandidier.

Distribution: Eastern and central Madagascar

Chamaeleo gallus

Description: Grows a flexible, scale-covered, blade-like ros- tral protuberance as long as its head. Head compressed and covered with smooth, small, polygonal shields. No parietal crest. A member of the *nasutus* group living in rain forests. Grows to 4 inches. First described by Günther, 1879.

Distribution: Eastern and north-central Madagascar

Chamaeleo gastrotaenia gastrotaenia

Description: Related to *C. furcifer* (Hillenius, 1959). Usually light green with a dull red stripe bordered in white running ventrally; front of the mouth cavity is yellow orange. Sometimes slate gray on top and dark purple below. Low casque; dorsal crest present. Length of 5 inches. First described by Boulenger, 1888.

Distribution: Madagascar, near Perinet

Chamaeleo gastrotaenia marojezensis

Description: Similar to *gastrotaenia* with the addition of a hint of a dorsal crest and very fine scales and slight growth on the upper "lip." First described by Brygoo, Blanc and Domergue, 1970.

Distribution: Massif du Marojezy, Madagascar

Chamaeleo globifer

Description: A member of the *parsonii* group. High, flat casque and absence of crests except for a low dorsal crest. Males have twin rostral appendices that terminate in global protuberances. A rain forest species and highland. Both sexes are green. Grows to 15 inches. Günther, 1879.

Distribution: East, including Antananarivo, and southeast Madagascar

Chamaeleo goetzei goetzei

Description: First described by Tornier, 1899.

Distribution: Ilolo, Rungwe Mountains, Tanzania

Chamaeleo goetzei nyikae
NYIKA CHAMELEON

Description: First described by Loveridge, 1953.

Distribution: Nyika Plateau, Malawi

Chamaeleo gracilis etiennei

Description: Differs from *C. gracilis gracilis* by lacking tarsal spurs. Less developed occipital lobes. First described by Schmidt, 1919.

C. globifer, *with a high, flat casque.*

Distribution: Gabon south to Angola

Chamaeleo gracilis gracilis
GRACEFUL CHAMELEON

Description: Closely related to *C. chamaeleon* and *dilepis* with comparatively small, immobile occipital lobes. Tarsal spurs present. Posterior casque elevation and noticeable lateral crest. Gular crest present. Yellow to blue-green coloration with a pale lateral band. Grows to 12 inches. First described by Hallowell, 1842.

Distribution: Somalia south to northern Tanzania and west to southern Cameroon and Senegal

Chamaeleo guentheri

Description: Considered a form of *C. pardalis.* First described by Boulenger, 1888; Angel, 1942.

Distribution: Madagascar

Chamaeleo guibei

Description: A member of the *nasutus* group. Separated occipital lobes and very short, scaled, flexible rostral appendix. No elevated casque or crests. Scia dentata present. Grows to 5 inches. First described by Hillenius, 1959.

Distribution: Northeastern Madagascar, Tsaratanana

Chamaeleo hoehnelii
HIGH-CASQUED CHAMELEON

Description: As the name implies, this diminutive chameleon has a high helmet or casque rising at the back of the skull. Pronounced gular crest and heterogeneous squamation. Lives in high forest up to snow-line. Grows to 6 inches. First described by Steindachner, 1891.

Distribution: Mt. Elgon and Aberdare Mountains of Kenya

Chamaeleo hoehnelii altaeelgonis

Description: Ovoviviparous. Roughly heterogeneous squamation, moderate to small size, parietal crest forked in front, gular crest and ventral crest, dorsal crest with unequal cones. First described by Loveridge, 1957, as *C. bitaeniatus altaeelgonis.* Given current name by Mertens, 1966.

Distribution: Mt. Elgon in northeastern Kenya

Chamaeleo incornutus

Description: May belong to the *bitaeniatus* group. Large occipital lobes, low dorsal crest of spinose scales. First described by Loveridge, 1932.

Distribution: Ukinge, Rungwe and Poroto Mountains of Tanzania

Chamaeleo jacksonii jacksonii
JACKSON'S CHAMELEON

Description: A large green lizard, the males sport three horns and resemble tiny Triceratops. Ovoviviparous. Roughly heterogeneous squamation, parietal crest forked in front, gular crest and ventral crest absent, dorsal crest with unequal cones. Grows to 12 inches. First described by Boulenger, 1896.

Distribution: Nairobi to Mt. Kenya (western and southwestern sides), Aberdare Mountains, Kenya and Usambara Mountains, Tanzania. Inconclusive reports place them in Uganda and northern Mozambique.

Chamaeleo jacksonii merumontana

Description: Ovoviviparous. Roughly heterogeneous squamation, moderate to small size, parietal crest forked in front, gular crest and ventral crest absent, dorsal crest with unequal cones. First described by Rand, 1958.

Distribution: Mt. Meru and Arusha District, Tanzania

Chamaeleo jacksonii xantholophus

Description: Ovoviviparous. Roughly heterogeneous squamation, moderate to small size, parietal crest forked in front and lightly colored, gular crest and ventral crest absent, dorsal crest with unequal cones. First described by Eason, Ferguson and Hebrand, 1988.

Distribution: Southern side of Mt. Kenya to the northeastern side of Mt. Meru

Chamaeleo johnstoni ituriensis
ITURI CHAMELEON

Description: Usually forest green with large, irregular black spots. Displays pale yellow green without spots, olive green marked with spots or dark brownish green without spots. No horns. Parietal crest more curved than *C. j. johnstoni.* Grows to 10 inches. First described by Schmidt, 1919.

Distribution: Central African Republic and eastern Zaire, including the Ituri Forest of the Pygmies

Chamaeleo johnstoni johnstoni
JOHNSTON'S CHAMELEON

Description: Three-horned chameleon, darker than a Jackson's with blue and light-green spots. Females don't develop horns. "Jumps" to the forest floor when threatened. No occipital lobes. Well-developed lateral crest. Tail about the same length as head and body combined. Grows to about 10 inches. First described by Boulenger, 1901.

Distribution: Uganda, Rwanda, Burundi and bordering Zaire

Chamaeleo karroicum

Description: Possesses a distinct but low casque with shallow cranial crests. Prominent gular and dorsal crests. Tail is

C. hoehnelii, *the high-casqued chameleon.*

Jackson's chameleon, C. jacksonii, *sports one rostral and two orbital horns.*

shorter than the head and body. Light gray and pale brown highlighted with grayish green. Sometimes rows of rust run along the flanks. Also known as *Bradypodion karroicum* or the Karoo dwarf chameleon. First described by Methuen and Hewill, 1915.

Distribution: Karoo region of South Cape Province, South Africa

Chamaeleo kinetensis

Description: Originally considered a subspecies of *ribitaeniatus*. First described by Schmidt, 1943.

Distribution: Imatong Mountains, Sudan

Chamaeleo labordi

Description: A one-horned chameleon. The horn is rigid and laterally compressed. Males have an elevated casque and a whitish lateral line on the side. Distinct dorsal crest. Both sexes have a white line under the tail contrasting with the predominant light green. May be a variety of *C. rhinoceratus. C. rhinoceratus voeltzkowi* is probably the same animal. Grows to 9 or 10 inches. First described by Grandidier, 1872.

Distribution: Coastal southwestern Madagascar, common along the Ihotry River

Chamaeleo lambertoni

Description: Same as *C. lateralis* except for the total absence of a gular crest. Called *C. lateralis* by Hillenius, 1959.

Distribution: Central and southern Madagascar

Chamaeleo lateralis
JEWEL CHAMELEON

Description: Double rows of scales on the dorsal keel, no occipital lobes and a white mid-ventral band. Usually has a single white stripe on the sides. Great variation in color. Parietal crest, lateral crest and distinct casque. Gular crest present. Adapts to many environments, from arid rock gardens to high, wet forest. Grows to 6 to 7 inches. First described by Gray, 1831.

Distribution: Throughout Madagascar excepting the north and northwest

Chamaeleo laterispinus

Description: First described by Loveridge, 1932.

Distribution: Uzungwe Mountains, Tanzania

Chamaeleo lavigularis

Description: First described by Müller, 1926. Considered the same as *C. johnstoni* by Mertens, 1966.

Distribution: South Africa

Chamaeleo linotus

Description: A member of the *nasutus* group, lacks dorsal crest. Only the male possesses a rostral appendix. Lives near 3,000-foot elevation. Grows to 5 inches. First described by Müller, 1924.

Distribution: Northeast Madagascar, Ambatodradama, Maroantsetra Province

Chamaeleo malthe

Description: A member of the *cucullatus* group closely resembling *brevicornis.* Fused occipital lobes and isolated cones under the throat and belly. Dorsal crest present. Males have a flat rostral appendix grooved above and below. Greenish yellow with white upper lip and blue-green occipital lobes. Grows to 12 inches. First described by Günther, 1879.

Distribution: Northern, central and eastern Madagascar

Chamaeleo melleri
MELLER'S CHAMELEON

Description: A leaf-green species with large, separated occipital lobes and a low forehead. Fin-shaped dorsal keel. This is the largest species in Africa, exceeding 2 feet. First described by Gray, 1864.

Distribution: Tanzania and southern Malawi

Chamaeleo minor

Description: Distinguished by a flat casque, absence of occipital lobes and single or paired white lines under the tail and one white stripe along the midventral line. Low dorsal crest. Dark green. Males have two rigid, short, laterally compressed rostral protuberances with the tips pointing out to the sides. Grows to about 6 inches. First described by Günther, 1879.

Distribution: South-central Madagascar

Chamaeleo mlanjensis
Description: First described by Broadley, 1965.

Distribution: Mlanje Mountains, Malawi

Chamaeleo monoceras

Description: A single-horned chameleon, possibly the same as *C. rhinoceratus*, with a lateral row of larger scales on the flanks and sometimes a whitish coloration under the tail. First described by Boettger, 1913.

Distribution: Northwestern Madagascar, Betsaleo near Mahajanga

Chamaeleo montium camerunensus
Description: Annulated horns. Described by Müller, 1909.

The brightly colored C. lateralis *is marked by a white band along its sides.*

Distribution: Cameroon

Chamaeleo montium feae

Description: First described by Boulenger, 1906.

Distribution: Bioko (Fernando Po) Island, Gulf of Guinea

Chamaeleo montium montium
MOUNTAIN or
CAMEROON SAIL-FIN CHAMELEON

Description: Males have a large fin-shaped dorsal keel and three annulate horns. Both sexes show a lateral row of larger shields on the flank and a double row of scales on the dorsal keel. Heterogeneous squamation. Ranges from 6 to 12 inches. First described by Buchholz, 1874.

Distribution: Buea and Mt. Cameroon, Cameroon

Chamaeleo namaquensis
NAMAQUA CHAMELEON

Description: Prominent dorsal crest and roof-shaped casque. Homogeneous squamation with scales sometimes arranged in rosettes. Lamellate soles, partly fringed toes, and

Two views of C. melleri, *the largest African chameleon species. Meller's chameleon has a speckled appearance and can grow to more than two feet in length.*

tail no longer than body length. Able to run from predators. Tail is not fully prehensile. Grayish green to bright maroon. Grows to 10 inches. First described by Smith, 1831.

Distribution: Western Cape Province, South Africa, to Gobabis and Namib Desert and Angola, generally along the coast

Chamaeleo nasutus

Description: Grows to just 3 inches, the smallest in the genus. Possesses a flexible, short, scale-covered rostral appendix. No parietal crest or occipital lobes. Scia dentata often present. Prefers sleeping within 3 to 6 feet of the ground. Usually light brown or gray green with variable dark bands on flank. First described by Dumeril and Bibron, 1836.

Distribution: Eastern Madagascar (including Perinet) and Isle St. Marie

Chamaeleo nemorale
ZULULAND DWARF CHAMELEON

Description: Recurved, prominent casque and modest cranial casque. Gular and dorsal crest present. Tail shorter than the body. Dark green with rust-colored blotches. Also known as *Bradypodion nemorale* or the Zululand dwarf chameleon. Grows to 6 inches. First described by Raw, 1978.

Distribution: Nklanda and Qudeni forests, Kwazulu

Chamaeleo oshaughnessyi
O'SHAUGHNESSY'S CHAMELEON

Description: A member of the *Parsonii* group, characterized by a high, flat casque, lack of crests, and two small, rigid rostral appendices. Dull green with blue-green highlights. Heterogeneous squamation. Can exceed 15 inches. First described by Günther, 1881.

Distribution: Northeast, east and south-central Madagascar

Chamaeleo oustaleti
OUSTALET'S CHAMELEON

Description: A contender for the largest chameleon, the Oustalet's grows to over 2 feet in length. Eats insects, birds and rodents. Drab colors. Very high casque. No occipital lobes or rostral appendage. Gular and dorsal crests present. Also called the helmeted chameleon or the Malagasy giant chameleon. Along with the *lateralis*, it is the most widespread species on the island, inhabiting all but the wettest regions. First described by Mocquard, 1894.

Distribution: Central, southwestern and northern third of Madagascar. Also introduced to the Ngong Forest near Nairobi, Kenya. North-central region is the center of distribution

Chamaeleo oweni
OWEN'S CHAMELEON

Description: A three-horned chameleon. Green coloration, marked by white, yellow, brown, reddish brown and black, depending on display. Deliberately falls from trees to flee. Small occipital lobes and distinct lateral crest. Females sometimes grow a single rostral horn. Tail much longer than head and body combined. Double row of scales on the dorsal keel. Very aggressive, even to humans. Grows to 14 inches. First described by Gray, 1831.

Distribution: Nigeria to the lowlands near Mt. Cameroon and toward Zaire

Chamaeleo pardalis
PANTHER CHAMELEON

Description: One of the most colorful chameleons (see p. 131). Prefers hot and humid regions. Strong parietal crest leads to a posteriorly elevated casque. Distinct lateral crest that leads to the canthi rostrales in both sexes. Dorsal, gular and ventral crests. Heterogeneous squamation. First described by Cuvier, 1829.

Distribution: Common on the east coast of Madagascar. Also found on the west and north coasts. Unusual colorations found on the island of Nosy Be. Introduced by man on St. Paul's Island, Réunion Island and possibly Mauritius

Chamaeleo parsonii christifer

Description: Essentially a *parsonii* with a low dorsal and incipient parietal crest. Grows to 11 inches. First described by Methuen, 1913.

C. m. montium, the sail-fin chameleon, has a characteristic dorsal keel and prominent horns.

Distribution: Environs of Perinet, Madagascar

Chamaeleo parsonii parsonii
PARSON'S CHAMELEON

Description: The head is larger in proportion to the rest of the animal, with a high flat casque and no parietal crest. No gular, ventral or dorsal crests. Color ranges from turquoise to green. Two rigid, flattened lateral protuberances on the males. Scia dentata present. Can exceed 2 feet in length. First described by Cuvier, 1824.

Distribution: Central, eastern Madagascar (north of Toamasina near Perinet), near Ambanja in the northeast and on Nosy Borah (St. Marie) Island

Chamaeleo peyrieresi

Description: First described by Brygoo, Blanc and Domergue.

Distribution: Madagascar

Chamaeleo pfefferi

Description: First described by Tornier, 1900.

Distribution: Cameroon

Chamaeleo polleni

Description: Lacks protuberances, conspicuous crests or occipital lobes. Homogeneous squamation. Grows to about 5 inches. First described by Peters, 1873.

Distribution: Mayotte Island, Comoro Islands

Chamaeleo pumilus caffer
BOETTGER'S DWARF CHAMELEON

Description: Lateral rows of larger scales on the flanks. Small, overlapping, compressed gular lobes. Dorsal crest consisting of large compressed tubercles extending along the tail in males. Mottled brown, olive and yellowish white. An irregular stripe runs laterally on the body. Lives in low coastal forest. Also known as *Bradypodion caffrum* or Transkei dwarf chameleon. Grows to 5 inches. First described by Boettger, 1889. Placed in the *pumilus* group by Hillenius, 1959.

Distribution: Port St. Johns area, Pondoland, eastern South Africa

Chamaeleo pumilus gutturalis
ROBERTSON'S DWARF CHAMELEON

Description: Cranial and dorsal crests and large gular lobes. Scattered, very large convex tubercles arranged in two irregular rows on the sides. Blue gray with rust and light orange markings. Also known as *Bradypodion gutterale* or the Robertson dwarf chameleon. Grows up to 6 inches. First described by Smith, 1849.

Distribution: Low elevations of Mt. Keromsberg, South Africa

Chamaeleo pumilus karrooicus
KARROO DWARF CHAMELEON

Description: Live birth. Low casque, lateral rows of larger scales on the flanks and large, scaled gular lobes. Drab gray and brown. Displaying males turn blue-black with bright rust stripes. Also known as *Bradypodion karroicum*. First described by Methuen and Hewitt, 1915.

This C. pardalis *has a reddish hue.*

A beautifully colored Parson's chameleon, C. parsonii.

C. oustaleti, *Oustalet's chameleon, may grow to
over 2 feet in length.*

At just 3 inches, C. nasutus *is the smallest of
the* Chamaeleo *genus.*

Distribution: Karroo areas of South Cape Province, South Africa

Chamaeleo pumilus melanocephalus
BLACK-HEADED DWARF CHAMELEON

Description: Minimal casque and cranial casque. Faint dorsal and gular crests. Tail slightly longer than head and body on the males. Green-brown coloration interrupted by two or three darker blotches. Grows to 4 inches. Also known as *Bradypodion melanocephalum* or the black-headed dwarf chameleon. First described by Gray, 1864. Confirmed by Hillenius, 1959.

Distribution: Coast of Pondoland through Natal, South Africa; Kwazulu to southern Mozambique

Chamaeleo pumilus occidentalis
NAMAQUA DWARF CHAMELEON

Description: Cranial crest, lateral rows of larger scales on flanks. Large, overlapping, scaled, compressed gular lobes. Drab gray and brown. Displaying males turn blue-black with bright rust stripes. Casque not narrowed and dorsal crest continuous. Also known as *Bradypodion occidentale.* First described by Hewitt, 1935.

Distribution: Luderitz, Namibia, to the coast of Great Namaqualand and south to Little Namaqualand

Chamaeleo pumilus pumilus
CAPE DWARF CHAMELEON

Description: Pale green. Displays a bright maroon or orange band on its side. Live birth. Lateral rows of larger scales on flank. Scaled and compressed gular lobes. Dorsal and gular crests present. Lives in coastal brush and reeds. Also known as *Bradypodion pumilum.* Reaches 4 to 6 inches in length. First described by Gmelin, 1789.

Distribution: Western Cape Province, South Africa

Chamaeleo pumilus taeniobronchus
SMITH'S DWARF CHAMELEON

Description: Live birth. Gular and dorsal crests composed of small tubercular cones. Dirty to pale green with black throat grooves. Some specimens are rust colored with maroon throat grooves. Lives atop mountains near the sea.

Also known as *Bradypodion taeniobronchum*. First described by Smith, 1831.

Distribution: Algoa Bay, Cape Province, South Africa

Chamaeleo pumilus transvaalensis
TRANSVAAL DWARF CHAMELEON

Description: Modest casque and conspicuous cranial crest. Large gular and dorsal crests. Tail is a little longer than the body. A yellow stripe bordered in maroon runs from the head to the flanks of the males. Live birth. Lives in wet forest on Transvaal escarpment ravines. Also known as *Bradypodion transvaalense*. Grows to 8 inches. First described by FitzSimons, 1930, and placed in the *pumilus* group by Hillenius, 1959.

Distribution: Transvaal and Swaziland

Chamaeleo pumilus ventralis

Description: Ovoviviparous. Lateral rows of larger scales on flanks. Large, overlapping, scaled, compressed gular lobes. Drab gray and brown. Displaying males turn blue-black with bright rust stripes. Casque narrow and pointed; dorsal crest prominent but discontinuous. Also known as *Bradypodion ventrale*. First described by Gray, 1845.

Distribution: Eastern Cape Province, South Africa

Chamaeleo quadricornis
FOUR-HORNED CHAMELEON

Description: Two moderate-sized rostral annulated horns with two smaller horns placed just above. Sail-fin dorsal crest. No occipital lobes. Prominent gular crest composed of long scales. Ventral crest. First described by Tornier, 1899.

Distribution: Mts. Manenguba and Lefo, Cameroon

Chamaeleo rhinoceratus rhinoceratus
RHINOCEROS CHAMELEON

Description: A one-horned chameleon. The horn is rigid and laterally compressed. Grows to 9 or 10 inches. Whitish lateral line on the side and sometimes a whitish coloration under the tail. Males have a dorsal crest. Homogeneous

Two views of the smooth-skinned Senegal chameleon,
C. senegalensis.

---

squamation. Orbital and dorsal crests. Very rare. First
described by Gray, 1845.

Distribution: Northwest, southwest and west Madagascar

Chamaeleo rhinoceratus voeltzkowi

Description: A small, single-horned chameleon. Probably the
same animal as *C. labordi.* First described by Boettger,
1893, or Grandidier, 1872.

Distribution: Southwest coast of Madagascar

Chamaeleo rudis rudis

Description: Irregular dorsal crest and even gular crest. Heterogeneous squamation; moderate casque. Found in many shades of green and reddish brown. Males have a slight rostral protuberance. Grows to 6 inches. First described by Boulenger, 1906.

Distribution: Uganda, Rwanda and bordering Zaire

Chamaeleo rudis schoutendeni

Description: First described by Laurent, 1952.

Distribution: Kabobo Mountains, Zaire

Chamaeleo rudis schubotzi

Description: First described by Sternfeld, 1912.

Distribution: Mt. Kenya

Chamaeleo rudis sternfeldi

Description: First described by Rand, 1963.

Distribution: Tanzania

Chamaeleo senegalensis
SENEGAL CHAMELEON

Description: This smooth-skinned chameleon is one of the most commonly imported species though it does very poorly in captivity. Well-developed lateral crest, noticeable gular crest and indistinct parietal crest. Color ranges from pale yellow to blue green to drab greenish brown. Grows to 10 inches. First described by Daudin, 1802.

Distribution: Sudan and Ethiopia, south to Uganda, Tanzania and Zambia, west to Angola and north to Togo and Senegal

Chamaeleo senegalensis laevigatus

Description: Closely related to the *Chamaeleo chamaeleon.* Small tarsal spurs. First described by Gray, 1863.

Distribution: Talanga Forest, southern Sudan

Chamaeleo setaroi
SETARO'S DWARF CHAMELEON

Description: Distinct, elevated casque and moderate cranial crests. Gular and dorsal crests have short flaps. Tail longer than the body in males. Dirty brown with orange stripes along the flanks. Throat pale green. Also known as *Bradypodion setoroi.* Grows to 4 or 5 inches. First described by Raw, 1976.

Distribution: Coastal dune forests of Kwazulu

Chamaeleo spinosus

Description: First described by Matschie, 1892.

Distribution: Usambara Mountains, Tanzania

Chamaeleo tempeli

Description: A member of Hillenius's *bitaeniatus* group. Ovoviviparous. Roughly heterogeneous squamation, moderate to small size, parietal crest forked in front, gular crest and ventral crest, dorsal crest with unequal cones. "V"-shaped gular squamation and large occipital lobes. First described by Tornier, 1899.

Distribution: Uzungwe, Ubene and Ukinga Mountains, Tanzania

Chamaeleo tenuis

Description: Small lizard with flattened rostral appendix in both sexes. Placed among *Bradypodion* by Klaver and Böhme, 1986, because of lung and hemipenis characters. First described by Matchie, 1892.

Distribution: Usambara Mountains, Tanzania

Chamaeleo thamnobates
NATAL MIDLANDS DWARF CHAMELEON

Description: Pronounced casque and cranial crest. Long gular and dorsal crests. Tail longer than the head and body in males. Males are blue green with a yellow or rust lateral patch. Scattered red scales. Females are gray to brown. Lives in forest and bush. Also known as *Bradypodion thamnobates.* Grows to 8 inches. First described by Raw, 1976.

Distribution: Natal Midlands, South Africa

Chamaeleo tigris
TIGER CHAMELEON

Description: Scaled chin lobe like *pumilus,* and forked parietal crest like *bitaeniatus.* Homogeneous squamation unlike either. If it proves to be ovoviviparous, scientists believe it may be an intermediate link between *bitaeniatus* and *pumilus,* the two chameleon groups that give live birth. Grows to 6 inches. First described by Kuhl, 1820.

Distribution: Seychelles Islands, including La Misère, Mahé Valée de Mai and Praslin

Chamaeleo tsaratananensis

Description: Reddish brown with heterogeneous squamation and long gular crest. Three large round scales on the occipital lobes. No dorsal crest. Similar but not identical to *C. malthe.* Grows to 4 inches. First described by Brygoo and Domergue, 1968.

Distribution: Near Tsaratanana in north-central Madagascar

Chamaeleo tuzentae

Description: First described by Brygoo, Bourgat, and Domergue, 1972.

Distribution: Southwestern Madagascar, Andrenalamivola, near Ambiky

Chamaeleo verrucosus semicristatus

Description: May be the same as verrucosus. First described by Boettger, 1894.

Distribution: Madagascar

Chamaeleo verrucosus verrucosus

Description: A member of Hillenius's *oustaleti* group. Highly elevated crest, no occipital lobes, prominent parietal crest and dorsal crest, no axial pits. Small gular crest. Grows to 22 inches. First described by Cuvier, 1829.

Distribution: Madagascar (except central areas), the Bourbon Islands and Mauritius. Center of distribution in southern and southwest Madagascar

Chamaeleo werneri

Description: A member of the *bitaeniatus* group. Ovovivipa-rous. Roughly heterogeneous squamation, moderate to small size, parietal crest forked in front, gular crest and

C. verrucosus has prominent parietal and dorsal crests.

C. willsii *displays short rostral protuberances.*

ventral crest, dorsal crest with unequal cones. "V"-shaped gular squamation and large occipital lobes. Males have three horns, females one rostral horn. First described by Tornier, 1899.

Distribution: Uluguru and Uzungwe Mountains, Tanzania

Chamaeleo wiedersheimi

Description: Dorsal knobs, temporal crest, lateral row of larger shields on the flank, and an indistinct groove on the upper lip from nostril to nostril. First described by Nieden, 1910.

Distribution: Mt. Lefo, northern Cameroon

Chamaeleo willsii petteri

Description: Green with a white ventral line. Homogeneous squamation with finer scales than willsii. The twin rostral protuberances in the males more closely resemble the larger bifidus than willsii. A rain forest species, some inhabit the forests bounded by the spiny limestone karst formations of the Ankarana massif. Grows to 5 inches. First described by Brygoo and Domergue, 1966.

Distribution: Joffreville near Diégo-Suarez and Ankarana

Chamaeleo willsii willsii

Description: Small crests. Green with yellow scales on the flanks. Distinguished by a flat casque, absence of occipital lobes, paired white lines under the tail and a single stripe along the midventral line. Males have two rigid, short, laterally compressed rostral protuberances. Inhabits the top of the canopy. Grows to 4 inches. First described by Günther, 1890.

Distribution: Eastern Madagascar near Perinet

Chamaeleo xenorhinus

Description: Bifurcated, spatulate rostral appendix on the males and small split nub on the females. Huge casque topped by curving parietal crest. Well-developed lateral crest. Heterogeneous squamation. Males are uniform olive; the females are brown. Grows to 11 inches. First described by Boulenger, 1901.

Distribution: Ruwenzori Mountains, Uganda and Zaire

GENUS BROOKESIA
Madagascar Stumptail or Leaf Chameleons

Brookesia antoetrae

Description: First described by Brygoo and Domergue, 1971.

Distribution: Madagascar

Brookesia betschii

Description: First described by Brygoo, Blanc and Domergue, 1974.

Distribution: Madagascar

Brookesia bonsi

Description: First described by Ramanantsoa, 1980.

Distribution: Northwest, in Reserve Naturelle No. 8, Tsingy de Namoroka, subprefecture of Soalala

Brookesia decaryi

Description: A plump animal with spines on its skull. First described by Angel, 1938.

Distribution: West coast, forest on the Ankarafantsika Massif

Brookesia dentata

Description: First described by Mocquard, 1900.

Distribution: Northwest, Suberbieville, south of Maevatanana

Brookesia ebenaui

Description: First described by Boettger, 1880.

Distribution: Northern third of the island, including Nosy Be and south down the central hills

Brookesia griveaudi

Description: Rectilinear lateral and praeorbital crests. First described by Brygoo, Blanc and Domergue, 1974.

Distribution: Northeast section, Marojejy

Brookesia karachi

Description: A small brown spindly-legged animal living in dense forest on the ground in dead leaves. Granular scales run along the spine. First described by Brygoo, Blanc and Domergue, 1970.

Distribution: Northeast Mt. Marojejy in Réserve Naturelle at about 2,200 feet

Brookesia lambertoni

Description: Very heterogeneous squamation. First described by Brygoo and Domergue, 1970.

Distribution: Fito, in Sihanaka

Brookesia legenderi

Description: First described by Ramanantsoa, 1980.

Distribution: Nosy Be, Réserve Naturelle

Brookesia minima

Description: The world's smallest chameleon, it grows to only a little over an inch in total length. First described by Boettger, 1893.

Distribution: Nosy Be

Brookesia nasus nasus

Description: Head elongated, capped with two conical, projecting scales. First described by Boulenger.

A mysterious, unidentified redhead.

Distribution: East, southeast and central Madagascar

Brookesia nasus pauliani

Description: First described by Brygoo, Blanc and Domergue, 1972.

Distribution: Madagascar

Brookesia peramata

Description: Lives below 1,000 feet in elevation. Lobes of skin at the back of its head and two parallel rows of thorny

Chamaeleo globifer

spines running down its back. Large rigid scales form pyramidal "rosettes" on the sides. Considered an example of a new genus, *Leandria*, by its discoverer. First described by Angel, 1933.

Distribution: Antsingy region, Menabe Province

Brookesia peyrieresi

Description: First described by Brygoo and Domergue, 1975.

Distribution: Northeast, Nosy Mangabe, Antongil Bay

Brookesia ramanantsoai

Description: First described by Brygoo and Domergue, 1975.

Distribution: Central Madagascar, Ambohiboataba Forest east of Mantasoa

Brookesia stumpffi

Description: Lives in forests under dry leaves and in rotten tree trunks. Spines on the head and back. A crenellated crest follows the upper curve of the orbit. A plate grows over the base of the tail on either side and is drawn into a spine. Grows to 3.5 inches. First described by Boettger, 1894.

Distribution: Western side of the island, including Nosy Be, and eastern side

Brookesia superciliaris

Description: Predominantly terrestrial. Light brown with no patterns. Males develop patterns on face during displays. Tail somewhat prehensile. Grows to 3.5 inches. First described by Kuhl, 1820.

Distribution: Northwest, northeast, east and southeast Nosy Be

Brookesia therezieni

Description: Groups of horizontal spines underneath the tail. First described by Brygoo and Domergue, 1970.

Distribution: Eastern Madagascar, Perinet

Brookesia thieli

Description: A brown band runs along the spine. Distinct chin scales present. Active in the day. Lives on the ground or among bushes in forested areas at elevations between 3,000 and 4,500 feet. First described by Brygoo and Domergue, 1969.

Distribution: Eastern Madagascar, Moramanga and Maroantsetra subprefectures, including Perinet

Brookesia tuberculata

Description: Similar in size and morphology to *B. minima.* First described by Mocquard, 1894.

Distribution: North, on Mt. d'Ambre

Brookesia vadoni

Description: A series of vertical spines on the upper part of the tail. First described by Brygoo and Domergue, 1968.

Distribution: Northwest, the valley of Iaraka River, near Masoala, at elevations between 1,500 and 3,000 feet

GENUS RHAMPHOLEON
African Stumptail or Leaf Chameleons

Rhampholeon brachyrus
Description: First described by Günther, 1892.
Distribution:

Rhampholeon brachyrus lonidesi
Description: First described by Loveridge, 1951.
Distribution:

Rhampholeon brevicaudatus
Description: First described by Matschie, 1892.
Distribution: Coastal Tanzania

Rhampholeon carpenteri
Description: High spatulate casque
Distribution: Central Africa

Rhampholeon kerstenii
Description: First described by Peters, 1868.
Distribution: Kenya and Tanzania

Chamaeleo globifer

Rhampholeon kerstenii robecchii

Description: First described by Boulenger.

Distribution: Eastern Africa

Rhampholeon marshalli gorowgosae

Description: First described by Broadly, 1971.

Distribution: Mozambique

Rhampholeon marshalli marshalli

Description: Also called a leaf chameleon for its shape. Grows to 3 inches. Rostral appendage and knots of tubercles along the back. No crests, bulbous torso and a "low forehead." Brown to light green. Lives among leaves on the forest floor. First described by Boulenger, 1906.

Distribution: South Africa and Mozambique

Rhampholeon nchisiensis

Description: First described by Loveridge, 1953.

Distribution: Southern Africa

Rhampholeon platyceps carri

Description: First described by Loveridge, 1953.

Distribution: Malawi

Rhampholeon platyceps platyceps

Description: Flat-topped head covered with granular scales. Grows to 3 inches. First described by Günther, 1882.

Distribution: Malawi

Rhampholeon spectrum

Description: Tiny rostral appendix. Slightly elevated casque with well-developed lateral crest festooned with tubercles. Greenish brown, reddish brown or light gray. Grows to 3 inches. First described by Buchholz, 1874.

Distribution: Western Kenya, Tanzania, Burundi and Uganda; Eastern Zaire; Cameroon

Rhampholeon temporalis

Description: First described by Matschie, 1892.

Distribution: Usambara Mountains of Tanzania

GLOSSARY

acrodont Having teeth "soldered" onto the jawbone.

amphisbidians A suborder of limbless, burrowing reptiles in the order Squamata.

annulate Consisting of ring-like segments.

arboreal Living in trees.

axillary Near the armpit or shoulder.

bicuspid claw A claw having two points like a crescent moon.

biodiversity Having a wide range of species.

calyces A network of depressions found on the surface of hemipenes.

canthal crest A crest running toward the snout from below the eyes. The protrusions at the end of the crest are called canthi rostrale or rostral protuberances.

carotid body A chemoreceptor located in the arteries of the neck (carotid arteries) that responds to oxygen levels in the blood to help regulate respiration.

chromatophore Pigment-containing cells in the skin whose color can be changed by expansion or contraction in response to some stimuli.

chromosomes Thread-like structures in the nuclei of a cell that carry the genes.

cloaca The excretory and reproductive orifice.

clutch A group of eggs deposited at one time.

cold-blooded Having a body temperature that fluctuates according to the temperature of the surrounding air, land or water. Compare with endothermic.

crest A bony or scaly extrusion.

dermal Related to skin.

dorsal Pertaining to the top or back of an animal, e.g., a dorsal crest runs along the top of an animal's back.

endemic Pertaining to a native or localized population.

endothermic Having a nearly constant body temperature; warm-blooded.

epiphysis Part of the brain found near the frontal base of the skull.

family In taxonomy, a group of related genera. Similar families are grouped into orders. Chameleons are members of the Chamaeleonidae family.

genus In taxonomy, a group of related species. Similar genera are grouped into families. Depending upon which system of classification is used, there are at least two, and perhaps six, genera of chameleons.

glossohyal A large tongue muscle.

gular crest Crest found under the neck.

hemipenes The paired sex organ in male reptiles, including snakes and lizards.

heterogeneous squamation Having an arrangement of scales in varied colors or patterns.

homogeneous squamation Having an arrangement of scales in a uniform color or pattern.

hydrophobic Repelling moisture.

interstitial A thin layer between other layers.

Jacobson's organ A pair of organs on the roof of the mouth used to smell the contents of the mouth in conjunction with the tongue.

keratin   Hard, fibrous proteins that form the outer covering or shell of an animal.

lateral   Pertaining to the side of a body; e.g., a lateral crest runs along the side of the skull.

montane   Pertaining to a mountainous environment or species.

morphology   The structure and form of an organism.

nematodes   A large group of parasitic invertebrates, the roundworms.

occipital   Pertaining to the lower, posterior part of the skull; therefore, occipital lobes extrude from the back of the skull.

ontogeny   The course of development of a single organism.

orbital   Pertaining to the area around the eyes.

order   In taxonomy, a group of related families. Similar orders form a class. Chameleons are members of the class Reptilia, the order Squamata and the suborder Sauria.

osteology   The anatomical study of bones.

oviparous   Pertaining to animals in which the female lays eggs, which then develop outside the mother's body. Most chameleons are either oviparous or ovoviviparous.

ovoviviparous   Pertaining to animals in which eggs are produced and retained within the body of the female during their development. When the offspring are near term, the female lays the eggs, which hatch soon after. Most chameleons are ovoviviparous or oviparous.

parallel evolution   The development of similar structures independently in two or more animals.

parietal   Pertaining to the top of the head or forehead. A parietal crest is a bony ridge running vertically up the middle of the forehead.

peripheral dermal vasomotor control   Controlling bloodflow to the surface of the skin.

phylogeny   The evolutionary development of an organism.

praeorbital   Above the eye.

prehensile   Able to grip. Many chameleon species have prehensile tails, which wind around tree branches to assure a
firm hold.

rostral   Pertaining to the front of the head. Many chameleons
have beak-like or snout-like rostral projections or horns.

scia dentata   Scales around the mouth that look like teeth.

septa   Walls or membranes separating two body cavities.

sinus   A bodily cavity or channel, such as the nasal sinuses.

spatulate   Having a broad, flat shape.

species   In taxonomy, a group of animals that are capable of
breeding. Related species are grouped into genera. Some
species are further divided into subspecies.

spinose   Having a spine.

Squamata   The order of scaly reptiles that includes snakes,
lizards, amphisbidians.

squamation   The arrangement of scales.

stereoscopic vision   The ability to see depth by using two eyes
simultaneously.

tarsal spur   A thorn-like barb found above the ankle of the rear
leg.

taxonomy   The science of classifying organisms into catego-
ries, such as species, genera and families.

terrestrial   Dwelling on the ground or on land.

thermoregulation   The ability to regulate internal body temperature among cold-blooded animals.

tubercles   A small, round prominence on the skin.

ventral   Pertaining to the underside or belly of an animal.

vestigial   Of an anatomic structure.

viviparous   Pertaining to animals in which offspring develop
inside the body of the female, who then gives live birth.
Some chameleons are ovoviviparous, not truly viviparous.

BIBLIOGRAPHY

Abu-Ghalyun, Y., Greenwald, L. Hetherington, T.E., and Gaunt, A.S., "The Physiological Basis of Slow Locomotion in Chameleons," *Journal of Experimental Zoology*, 245:3 (1988), 225–231.

Bourgat, R.M, "Biogeographical Interest of *Chamaeleo pardalis* Cuvier, 1829 (Reptilia, Squamata, Chamaeleonidae) on Reunion Island," *Herpetologica*, 28:1 (1972), 22–24.

Branch, B., *Bill Branch's Field Guide to the Snakes and other Reptiles of Southern Africa*. London: New Holland, 1988; 179–187.

Brygoo, E.R., *Faune de Madagascar, XXXIII, Reptiles Sauriens Chamaeleonidae*. Paris: O.R.S.T.O.M. and C.N.R.S., 1971.

Buckley, R., "Experiment with Habitat Trees: Notes on the Captive Management of Chameleons," *Vivarium*, 3:3 (1991).

Burrage, B.R., "Comparative Ecology and Behavior of Chamaeleo pumilus pumilus (Gmelin) & C. namaquensis A. Smith (Sauria: Chamaeleonidae)," *Annals of the South African Museum*, 61 (1973), 1–158.

Bustard, H.R., "The Comparative Behavior of Chameleons: Fight Behavior in *Chamaeleo gracilis hallowell*," *Herpetologica*, 23:1 (1967), 44–50.

———. "Keeping and Breeding Oviparous Chameleons," *The British Herpetological Society Bulletin*, 27 (Spring 1989), 20–33.

———. "Notes on Growth, Sloughing, Feeding, Mating, Gestation, Lifespan, and Poor Health of Chameleons in Captivity," *Copeia*, 1963, 704–706.

———. "Observations on the Life History and Behavior of *Chamaeleo bitaeniatus fischer*," *Herpetologica*, 22:1 (1966), 13–23.

———. "Observations on the Life History of *Chamaeleo hoehnelii* (Steindachner)," *Copeia*, 4 (1965), 401–410.

DeWitt, C., "Jackson's Chameleons, *Chamaeleo jacksonii:* Captive Behavior, Care and Breeding," *The Viviarium*, 1:2 (1988), 17-20.

de Witte, G., *Les Chameleons de L'Afrique Centrale*. Turvuren, Belgium: Musee Royal de L'Afrique Centrale, 1965; Annales, Serie; In 8, Sciences Zoologiques, No. 142.

Dowling, H.G., "Color Change: Chameleon Camouflage," *Natural History*, February 1964, 40–43.

Eason, P., Ferguson, G.W., Hebrard, J., "Variation in *Chamaeleo jacksonii* (Sauria, Chamaeleontidae): Description of a New Subspecies," *Copeia*, 3 (1988), 580-590.

Gans, C., "The Chameleon," *Natural History*, April 1967, 53–59.

Grow, D., "How They Do It: Chameleons," *Zoo Life*, 2:4 (Fall 1991), 62–71.

Grzimeke, H.C., "Agamids and Chameleons" in *Grzimeke's Animal Life Encyclopedia*, Vol. 6: *Reptiles*. New York: Van Nostrand Reinhold, 1984; 227–241.

Haas, G., "Jacobson's Organ in the Chameleon," *Journal Morp. Phila.*, 81 (1947), 195–202.

Hebrard, J.J. and Madsen, T., "Dry Season Intersexual Habitat Partitioning by Flap-necked Chameleons (Chamaeleo dilepis) in Kenya," *Biotropica*, 16:1 (1984), 69–72.

Hillenius, D., "The Differentiation Within the Genus *Chamaeleo laurenti*, 1768," *Beaufortia*, 8:89 (1959), 1–92.

———. "Notes on Chameleons I—Comparative Cytology: Aid and New Complications in Chameleon-taxonomy," *Beaufortia*, 9:108 (1963), 201–218.

————. "Notes on Chameleons II—*Chamaeleo laevigularis*, a Synonym of *Chamaeleo johnstoni*," *Beaufortia*, 10:117 (1963), 44–47.

————. "Notes on Chameleons III—The Chameleons of Southern Arabia," *Beaufortia*, 13:156 (1966), 91–108.

————. "Notes on Chameleons V—The Chameleons of North Africa and Adjacent Countries, *Chamaeleo chameleon*," *Beaufortia*, 28:345 (1978), 37–54.

————. "The Relationship of Brookesia, Rhampholeon and Chamaeleo (Chamaeleonidae, Reptilia)," *Bijdragen Tot De Dierkunde*, 56:1 (1986), 29–38.

————. "The Skull of *Chamaeleo nasutus* Adds More Information to the Relationship of Chamaeleo with Rhampholeon and Brookesia," *Bijdragen Tot De Dierkunde*, 58:1 (1988), 7–11.

Hillenius, D. and Gasperetti, J., "Reptiles of Saudi Arabia: The Chameleons of Saudi Arabia," *Fauna of Saudi Arabia*, 6 (1984).

Klaver, C., "Lung-morphology in the Chamaeleonidae and its Bearing Upon Phylogeny, Systematics, and Zoogeography," *Z. Zool. Syst. Evolutionforshung*, 19 (1981), 36–58.

————. "A Review of *Brookesia* Systematics with Special Reference to Lung-morphology (Reptilia: Sauria: Chamaeleonidae)," *Bonner Zooligische Beitr.*, 30:1–2 (1979), 162–175.

Klaver, C. and Böhme, W., "Phylogeny and Classification of the Chamaeleonidae (Sauria) with Special Reference to Hemipenis Morphology," *Bonner Zooligische Monographien*, 22 (1986), 1–64.

————. "Systematics of *Bradypodion tenue* (Matschie, 1892) with a Description of a New Species from the Uluguru and Uzungwe Mountains, Tanzania," *Bonner Zooligische Beitr.*, 39:4 (November 1988), 381–393.

Lin, J., "Dessication Tolerance and Thermal Maxima in the Lizards, *Chamaeleo jacksoni* and *Chamaeleo hoehnelii*," *Copeia*, 2 (1980).

Linnaeus, C., *System Natura*. Tenth ed., 1758.

Marshall Cavendish International Wildlife Encyclopedia "Chameleon" 1989: 546–548.

Martin, J., "Chameleons: Now You See 'Em Now You Don't," *Smithsonian*, 21:3 (June 1991), 44–53.

Murphy, R.O., "The Most Amazing Tongue in Nature," *Natural History*, 45:5 (1940), 260–263.

Olgivie, P.W. and Owen, D.F., "Color Change and Polymorphism in *Chamaeleo bitaeniatus*," *Nature*, 202 (1964), 209–210.

Parcher, S.R., "Observations on the Natural Histories of Six Malagasy Chamaeleonidae," *Z. Tierpsychol.*, 34 (1974), 500–523.

Rand, A.S., "A Suggested Function of the Ornamentation of East African Forest Chameleons," *Copeia*, 4 (1961), 411–414.

Raw, L.R.G., "A Survey of the Dwarf Chameleons of Natal, South Africa, with Descriptions of Three New Species (Sauria: Chamaeleonidae)," 11:7 (1976), 139–161.

Rieppel, O., "The Phylogenetic Relationships Within the Chamaeleonidae with Comments on Some Aspects of Cladistic Analysis," *Zoological Journal of the Linnean Society*, 89:1 (1987), 41–62.

Schwenk, K. and Bell, D.A, "A Cryptic Intermediate in the Evolution of Chameleon Tongue Projection," *Experentia*, 44:8 (1988), 697–700.

Toxopeus, A.G., Kruijt, J.P, Hillenius, D, "Pair Bonding in Chameleons," *Naturwissenschaften*, 75:5 (1988), 268–269.

Wever, E.G., "The Ear of the Chameleon: *Chamaeleo senegalensis* and *Chamaeleo quilensis*," *The Journal of Experimental Zoology*, 168:4 (1968), 423–435.

———. "The Ear of the Chameleon: The Round Window Problem," *The Journal of Experimental Zoology*, 171:1 (1969), 1–5.

Zoond, A., "The Mechanism of Projection of the Chameleon's Tongue," *The Journal of Experimental Zoology*, 10 (1933), 174–185.

Zoond, A. and Eyre, J., "Studies in Reptilian Colour Response. I. The Bionomic and Physiology of the Pigmentary Activity of the Chamaeleon," *Phil. Trans. R. Soc.*, (B)223 (1934), 27–55.

———. "Studies in Reptilian Colour Response. II. The Role of Retinal and Dermal Photoreceptors in the Pigmentary Activity of the Chamaeleon," *The Journal of Experimental Biology*, 12 (1935), 39–43.

INDEX OF COMMON NAMES

AFRICAN CHAMELEON
Chamaeleo africanus

BLACK-HEADED DWARF
    CHAMELEON
*Chamaeleo pumilus
melancephalus*

BOETTGER'S CHAMELEON
Chamaeleo boettgeri

BOETTGER'S DWARF
    CHAMELEON
Chamaeleo pumilus caffer

CAPE DWARF CHAMELEON
Chamaeleo pumilus pumilus

COMMON OR EUROPEAN
    CHAMELEON
*Chamaeleo chameleon
chameleon*

CRESTED CHAMELEON
Chamaeleo cristatus

DRAKENSBERG DWARF
    CHAMELEON
*Chamaeleo pumilus
dracomontanum*

FISCHER'S CHAMELEON
Chamaeleo fischeri fischeri

FLAP-NECKED or COMMON
    CHAMELEON
Chamaeleo dilepis dilepis

FORK-NOSED CHAMELEON
Chamaeleo furcifer

FOUR-HORNED CHAMELEON
Chamaeleo quadricornis

GRACEFUL CHAMELEON
Chamaeleo gracilis gracilis

HIGH-CASQUE CHAMELEON
Chamaeleo hoehnelii

ITURI CHAMELEON
Chamaelo johnstoni ituriensis

JACKSON'S CHAMELEON
Chamaeleo jacksonii jacksonii

JEWEL CHAMELEON
Chamaeleo lateralis

JOHNSTON'S CHAMELEON
*Chamaeleo johnstoni
johnstoni*

KARROO DWARF
CHAMELEON
*Chamaeleo pumilus
karroicum*

KNYSNA DWARF
CHAMELEON
*Chamaeleo pumilus
damaranus*

MELLER'S CHAMELEON
Chamaeleo melleri

MOUNTAIN or CAMEROON
CHAMELEON
*Chamaeleo montium
montium*

NAMAQUA CHAMELEON
Chamaeleo namaquensis

NAMAQUA DWARF
CHAMELEON
*Chamaeleo pumilus
occidentalis*

NATAL MIDLANDS DWARF
CHAMELEON
Chamaeleo thamnobates

NYIKA CHAMELEON
Chamaeleo goetzei nyikae

O'SHAUGHNESSY'S
CHAMELEON
Chamaeleo oshaughnessyi

OUSTALET'S CHAMELEON
Chamaeleo oustaleti

OWEN'S CHAMELEON
Chamaeleo oweni

PANTHER CHAMELEON
Chamaeleo pardalis

PARSON'S CHAMELEON
Chamaeleo parsonii parsonii

RHINOCEROS CHAMELEON
*Chamaeleo rhinoceratus
rhinoceratus*

ROBERTSON'S DWARF
CHAMELEON
Chamaeleo pumilus gutturalis

SENEGAL CHAMELEON
Chamaeleo senegalensis

SETARO'S DWARF
CHAMELEON
Chamaeleo setaroi

SHORT-HORNED
CHAMELEON
*Chamaeleo brevicornis
brevicornis*

SMITH'S DWARF
CHAMELEON
*Chamaeleo pumilus
taeniobronchus*

TIGER CHAMELEON
Chamaeleo tigris

TRANSVAAL DWARF
CHAMELEON
*Chamaeleo pumilus
transvaalensis*

TWO-LINED CHAMELEON
*Chamaeleo bitaeniatus
bitaeniatus*

ZULULAND DWARF
CHAMELEON
Chamaeleo nemorale

INDEX OF SCIENTIFIC NAMES

Chamaeleo brevicornis hilleniusi

Chamaeleo brevicornis tsarafidyi

Chamaeleo calyptratus

Chamaeleo calyptratus calcarifer

Chamaeleo campani

Chamaeleo capuroni

Chamaeleo carpenteri

Chamaeleo cephalolepis

Chamaeleo chamaeleon arabicus

Chamaeleo chameleon chameleon

Chamaeleo chameleon musae

Chamaeleo chamaeleon orientalis

Chamaeleo chamaeleon recticrista

Chamaeleo chamaeleon zeylanicus

Chamaeleo chapini

Chamaeleo cristatus

Chamaeleo cucullatus

Chamaeleo damaranus

Chamaeleo deremensis

Chamaeleo dilepsis dilepsis

Chamaeleo dilepsis idjwiensis

Chamaeleo dilepsis isabellinus

Chamaeleo dilepsis petersii

Chamaeleo dilepsis quilensis

Chamaeleo dilepsis roperi

Chamaeleo dilepsis ruspolii

Chamaeleo dracomontanum

Chamaeleo eisentrauti

Chamaeleo fallax

Chamaeleo fischeri excubitor

Chamaeleo fischeri fischeri

Chamaeleo fischeri multituberculatus

Chamaeleo fischeri tavetanus

Chamaeleo fischeri uluguruensis

Chamaeleo fischeri uthmolleri

Chamaeleo fuelleborni

Chamaeleo furcifer

Chamaeleo gallus

Chamaeleo gastrotaenia gastrotaenia

Chamaeleo gastrotaenia marojezensis

Chamaeleo globifer

Chamaeleo goetzei goetzei

Chamaeleo goetzei nyikae

Chamaeleo gracilis etiennei

Chamaeleo gracilis gracilis

Chamaeleo guentheri

Chamaeleo guibei

Chamaeleo hoehnelii

Chamaeleo hoehnelii altaeelgonis

Chamaeleo incornutus

Chamaeleo jacksonii jacksonii

Chamaeleo jacksonii merumontana

Chamaeleo jacksonii xantholophus

Chamaeleo johnstoni ituriensis

Chamaeleo johnstoni johnstoni

Chamaeleo karroicum

Chamaeleo kinetensis

Chamaeleo labordi

Chamaeleo lambertoni

Chamaeleo lateralis

Chamaeleo laterispinus

Chamaeleo lavigularis

Chamaeleo linotus

Chamaeleo malthe

Chamaeleo melleri

Chamaeleo minor

Chamaeleo mlanjensis

Chamaeleo monoceras

Chamaeleo montium camerunensus

Chamaeleo montium feae

Chamaeleo montium montium

Chamaeleo namaquensis

Chamaeleo nasutus

Chamaeleo nemorale

Chamaeleo oshaughnessyi

Chamaeleo oustaleti

Chamaeleo oweni

Chamaeleo pardalis

Chamaeleo parsonii christifer

Chamaeleo parsonii parsonii

Chamaeleo petteri

Chamaeleo peyrieresi

Chamaeleo pfefferi

Chamaeleo polleni

Chamaeleo pumilus caffer

Chamaeleo pumilus gutturalis

Chamaeleo pumilus karrooicus

Chamaeleo pumilus melanocephalus

Chamaeleo pumilus oc-cidentalis

Chamaeleo pumilus pumilus

Chamaeleo pumilus taeniobronchus

Chamaeleo pumilus transvaalensis

Chamaeleo pumilus ventralis

Chamaeleo quadricornis

Chamaeleo rhinoceratus rhinoceratus

Chamaeleo rhinoceratus voeltzkowi

Chamaeleo rudis rudis

Chamaeleo rudis schoutendeni

Chamaeleo rudis schubotzi

Chamaeleo rudis sternfeldi

Chamaeleo senegalensis

*Chamaeleo senegalensis
laevigatus*

Chamaeleo setaroi

Chamaeleo spinosus

Chamaeleo tempeli

Chamaeleo tenuis

Chamaeleo thamnobates

Chamaeleo tigris

Chamaeleo tsaratananensis

Chamaeleo tuzentae

*Chamaeleo verrucosus semi-
cristatus*

*Chamaeleo verrucosus ver-
rucosus*

Chamaeleo werneri

Chamaeleo wiedersheimi

Chamaeleo willsii petteri

Chamaeleo willsii willsii

Chamaeleo xenorhinus

Rhampholeon brachyrus

Rhampholeon brevicaudatus

Rhampholeon carpenteri

Rhampholeon kerstenii

*Rhampholeon kerstenii
robecchii*

*Rhampholeon marshalli
gorowgosae*

*Rhampholeon marshalli
marshalli*

Rhampholeon nchisiensis

Rhampholeon platyceps carri

*Rhampholeon platyceps
platyceps*

Rhampholeon spectrum

Rhampholeon temporalis

C. lateralis.

INDEX

Page numbers in italics refer to illustrations

reptiles, chameleon's relation to other (table), 5
retractor muscles (tongue), 34
Rhampholeon (genus), 3, 9, 94
   R. brachyrus, 145
   R. brachyrus lonidesi, 145
   R. brevicaudatus, 145
   R. carpenteri, 145
   R. kerstenii, 145
   R. kerstenii robecchii, 146
   R. marshalli gorowgosae, 146
   R. marshalli marshalli, 146
   R. nchistiensis, 147
   R. platyceps carri, 147
   R. platyceps platyceps, 147
   R. spectrum, 147
   R. temporalis, 147
Rhinoceratus group (genus *Chamaeleo*), 92
rhinoceros chameleon (*Chamaeleo rhinoceratus rhinoceratus*), 133–134
Robertson's dwarf chameleon (*Chamaeleo pumilus gutturalis*), 129
rostral protuberances, 36

S

sail-fin chameleon, *30*
Sauria (suborder), 5, 6
scales, 16–17
scia dentata, 17
scientific names (list), 165–168
Senegal chameleon (*Chamaeleo senegalensis*), *134*, 136
senses, 28–29, 32–34
Setaro's dwarf chameleon (*Chamaeleo setaroi*), 136
shedding, 16–17, *18–19*
short-horned chameleon (*Chamaeleo brevicornis brevicornis*), 104
skin, 16–17—*See also coloration*
Smith's dwarf chameleon (*Chamaeleo pumilus taeniobronchus*), 132–133
snakes, 5, 24, 29
Somalia, xiv
South Africa, 7, 77–79
species-by-species list
   genus *Chamaeleo*, 98–140
   genus *Brookesia*, 140–145
   genus *Rhampholeon*, 145–147
sperm, 24
Squamata (order), 4–5
squamation, 16, *16*
   heterogeneous, 17
   homogeneous, 17
Sri Lanka, 49

stereoscopic vision, 32
stumptail chameleon, 8–9, *10–11*
superstitions—*See myths*

T

tail
   arboreal chameleons, 4
   Chamaeleo, 8
   prehensile, *6*, 8
Tanzania, xiv
tarsal spurs, 8
taxonomy, 7–9
   Hillenius's vs. Klaver's methods, 20–27
   Klaver's classification (chart), 26
territoriality—*See also defense*
   color, 40
   high-casqued chameleon, 71, 74
   panther chameleon, 64, 66
thermoregulation
   dwarf chameleon, 79–80
   high-casqued chameleon, 70
   Namaqua chameleon, 56–58
tiger chameleon (*Chamaeleo tigris*), 137
toes
   bundled, *7*, 8
   Chamaeleo, 8
   Rhampholeon, 9
tongue, 28–29, 32–34, *33*, 36
   dwarf chameleon, 81
   Parson's chameleon, *27*
Transvaal dwarf chameleon (*Chamaeleo pumilus transvaaensis*), 133
Tremper, Marilyn, 66
Tremper, Ron, 66, 68
Triceros (genus), 95
Tuatara, 5
tubercles, 17
turtles, 4
two-lined chameleon (*Chamaeleo bitaeniatus bitaeniatus*), 101

V

vision, 29, 32
vomeronasal organ (Jacobson's organ), 29

W

walking, 4

Z

Zululand dwarf chameleon (*Chamaeleo nemorale*), 126